D1457517

LORD MELBOURNE

LORD MELBOURNE

DOROTHY MARSHALL

INTRODUCTION BY
A.J.P. TAYLOR

WEIDENFELD AND NICOLSON
LONDON

Designed by Behram Kapadia
for George Weidenfeld and Nicolson Ltd

ISBN 0 297 76773 9

Printed in Great Britain by
Butler & Tanner Ltd, Frome and London

CONTENTS

ILLUSTRATIONS

Between pages 84 and 85

William Lamb painted by Hoppner (By gracious permission of H.M. the Queen)

Brocket Hall, Hertfordshire in 1786 (Mary Evans Picture Library)

Melbourne House, Whitehall in 1797 (British Library)

Emily Lamb, painted by Lawrence (By courtesy of Lord Mountbatten of Burma)

Lady Caroline Lamb (Mary Evans Picture Library)

William Lamb, painted by Lawrence (Mary Evans Picture Library)

Drawings from the sketchbook of Caroline Lamb (By courtesy of Henry Blyth Esq.)

Caroline Norton (Mary Evans Picture Library)

The House of Commons in 1821 (Department of the Environment; Crown Copyright Reserved)

Queen Victoria riding with Melbourne and Palmerston (National Portrait Gallery)

Cartoon of Victoria on the political see-saw (British Library)

Cartoon of Victoria accepting the hand of Prince Albert with Melbourne's approval (British Library)

INTRODUCTION

QUEEN VICTORIA, succeeding to the throne at the age of eighteen, was fortunate in her prime minister. Lord Melbourne had incomparable gifts as a lady's man. He was courteous, considerate, entertaining, willing to spend many happy hours with the admiring girl who was also his Queen. His entire life seemed to have been a preparation for the enchanted four years at the end of his career. In everything except his relations with Queen Victoria he is the most puzzling of British prime ministers.

Why on earth did Melbourne do it? He had little appetite for power. Indeed he made scarcely any attempt to wield power while he was in office. He was indifferent to popular applause. Ambition was the last emotion one could discover in him. He was not passionate about some cause or creed. He was a Whig Prime Minister, but if one attempted to set down what he meant by Whiggism it would turn out to be little more than good manners and scepticism about the value of political activity. Melbourne did not relish the glamour of his position. He did not attach great importance to its rewards. It is true that in old age he worried about his finances and believed he was ruined. Perhaps the fun of levying tribute on the public amused him. When he was Home Secretary, a little boy, the son of one of his secretaries, was brought in to see him. Melbourne pulled open a drawer full of pencils and india-rubbers, and said to the boy: 'Take as many as you like. They all belong to the public, and you can't get into the habit too soon of laying your hands on them.' It was his most memorable remark.

Melbourne found office a bore and then found being turned out of office a bore also. Here perhaps is the explanation of his career. He drifted listlessly from one political commitment to the next, never really interested and yet reluctant to give up public life altogether. There was not much to be said in his favour except his charm and sweetness of character, but also there was not much to be said against him. He had a sad private life and bore its burdens without complaining. British politics were at their most intense during the age of reform. Melbourne lowered the temperature by showing that he at any rate did not feel strongly about anything. I cannot see that he did much good in his life apart from contributing to Queen Victoria's political education. On the other hand I cannot see that he did much harm, and that was in itself a considerable achievement. On any other standard of judgement Melbourne remains to me a mysterious figure, delightful to read about, but what does he tell us about the political world in which prime ministers are supposed to rule supreme?

I

GROWING UP

THOUGH in the minds of most people Lord Melbourne's name is associated with that of Queen Victoria, the man himself neither in temperament nor in outlook remotely resembled the accepted picture of a well-bred Victorian gentleman. On the contrary he typified the century that was already passing into history as he grew into manhood; born in 1779, all his life he remained in essence a man of the eighteenth century, even to pronouncing Rome as Room and gold as gould. Though all men are, to a greater or lesser extent, the product of their environment, this was particularly true of William Lamb, the second Viscount Melbourne. It is idle to speculate as to what might have been his future had he not been born into a titled Whig family. With his well-cut features, expressive dark eyes, raven hair and well-built figure, his charm, enhanced by a melodious voice and uninhibited laugh, backed by his penetrating mind, he must have made his mark in some other way of life, but not through inclination in politics. It was circumstances that carried him, faintly resisting half the time, to the pinnacle of political power as Prime Minister of Britain. Melbourne was one of those men in England's story who apparently 'had greatness thrust upon them.'

His family background was typically eighteenth century. Society was hierarchical and exclusive; nevertheless it remained open ended. Men of ability could climb the social ladder via the accumulation of wealth and the possession of land, ascending first from the middling sort into gentility and then to the attainment of a modest title, a process that was normally the work of two or three generations. Neither the Lambs nor the methods by which they rose were exceptional. Even as early as Elizabethan England Cecil had recognised that the study of Law was the pathway of the ill-endowed to gentility and power and had recommended closing it to the low-born. So it proved to be for the Lambs. In the early eighteenth century a certain Peniston Lamb amassed a considerable fortune as a member of the Inns of Court, while his less ambitious brother followed the humbler calling of an attorney and legal adviser to the Cokes of Melbourne Hall in Derbyshire. The latter had two sons, one of whom became Bishop of Peterborough while the other, Mathew Lamb, also an attorney, continued to manage the Cokes' affairs. The details of his romance, if romance it was, have escaped the historian's net, though it is interesting to speculate as to whether it was solid worth, personal charm or the fortune which he inherited from his uncle, that won him the hand of Charlotte Coke, whom he married in 1740, and who on her brother's death succeeded to the Coke estates. The Lambs now entered the ranks of the landed gentry. Backed by ample means Mathew proceeded to enhance his consequence further by buying Brocket Hall in Hertfordshire. Here the future prime minister was to be born. Meanwhile Mathew took the next step up the social ladder; he bought a seat and went into Parliament, not because of any burning interest in politics but for the prestige which being a member brought. He made no personal mark in the Commons but in 1755 his steady support of the government was rewarded by a baronetcy. In a quiet way the Lambs had arrived.

When Mathew died he was reputed to be worth half a million, but though the possession of a baronetcy and a large fortune provided a solid foundation for further social advancement towards the ranks of the peerage, it was doubtful if his heir, another Peniston, left to himself would have done much more than fritter away the fortune which his father had accumulated. The drive, ability and ambition that had hitherto marked the rise of the Lamb family seem to have flickered out in young Peniston, who appeared content to lead the life of a man about town. Though he too entered Parliament he displayed neither industry nor talent in the world of politics. The next advance in the family fortunes was due to the remarkable woman he married in 1769. Elizabeth, the daughter of Sir Ralph Milbanke of Halnaby in Yorkshire, achieved a personal triumph in her rapid rise to the position of a leading London hostess. It is true that she had an excellent hand to play; she was something of a beauty, with dark expressive eyes and a shapely figure, attractions backed by her husband's wealth. Fortune favoured them in that after their marriage they were able to acquire the old Fox mansion in Piccadilly, which was no longer required by the Hollands whose headquarters were now Holland House in Kensington, where the formidable Lady Holland queened it over Whig society. Rechristened Melbourne House, this provided the Lambs with an elegant base for their sortie into London society. A fashionable artist was employed to paint the ceiling of the ballroom; young Lady Melbourne engaged first-rate cooks and kept an excellent table; soon the courtyard behind the great gates was full of elegant equipages. Nevertheless there were difficulties to be overcome. The pecking order among the aristocracy was well defined and the Lambs were a comparatively *nouveau riche* family. Wealth alone would not have been sufficient to push the colourless Peniston either into the ranks of the peerage or into a prominent position in London society; indeed not even with Lady Melbourne behind him could her pleasant ineffective husband achieve this.

Lady Melbourne was more than a wealthy attractive woman. She was also a very clever one, intelligent enough to know that though male admiration could be won by physical charms, an intelligent man needed an intelligent as well as a sympathetic listener if his admiration were to be more than transitory. Lady Melbourne was a realist with her feet planted on the ground, possibly part of her Yorkshire inheritance. She liked and understood men, and her flattery of them was that of a sophisticated woman of the world. Byron's comment on her later in life was 'If I had been a few years younger, what a fool she would have made of me, had she thought it worth her while.' She nearly did; despite her sixty years her influence over him was far from negligible. Nevertheless, though she preferred men and cultivated their company, she never made the mistake of antagonising their womenfolk. Shortly after the birth of their first son, another Peniston, in 1770, she was described as 'floating on the stream of fashionable life' in the company of the Duchess of Richmond and the gifted Mrs Damer. Sir Joshua Reynolds, who painted a charming portrait of her with her eldest son, tells how at a masquerade, then a fashionable amusement because the wearing of dominoes conferred a degree of anonymity, she, the Duchess of Ancaster and Lady Fordyce all appeared in dominoes as masculine looking as any macaroni. Nevertheless, gaily as Lady Melbourne indulged in the round of social pleasures, a well-disciplined ambition gave a pattern to her life. Gradually her husband gained the advancement that she had earned for him; in 1770 he reached the half-way house of an Irish peerage. Ireland at that time had her own Parliament and because Irish peers did not sit in the House of Lords, they were still eligible to stand for election to the English Commons. This meant that the conferring of Irish peerages was a convenient way of securing their support in that House while rewarding them for services already rendered there. To have got so far was gratifying and Lady Melbourne redoubled her efforts. In 1781 her husband was advanced to the rank of Viscount, though still in the Irish peerage. Finally her determined ambition was satisfied when in 1815 Peniston was given an English peerage.

It is interesting to speculate as to what extent the future prime minister was moulded by his parental heritage. Some qualities he clearly shared with his mother. He had her zest for life, a quality that she shared with all her children, combined with a capacity to accept people for what they were without being shocked by their inconsistencies and shortcomings. It was a foundation on which both tolerance and its ugly half-sister cynicism could be built, the former a quality which Melbourne tried to encourage in Queen Victoria without noticeable success. But one quality possessed by the mother was absent in the son. This was ambition. Without her drive the Lambs would never have achieved the social position that was to make it possible for a man of William's temperament to become prime minister. It was her ambition, and his lack of it, that explains how qualities basically similar in both could take such divergent paths. In both there was the same streak of earthy materialism, the same acceptance of human nature, but whereas Lady Melbourne used them to manipulate the people round her to serve her ends and promote her schemes, either for her own social advancement or for the interests of her family, in William the desire to manipulate was less than the indolence that made him more ready to observe and comment on the oddities of mankind than to use them. Even so, when in later life as prime minister he was dealing with difficult colleagues, he showed that he too had in no small measure this gift of using people. Lady Melbourne was hard-headed, though good-natured and kindly enough when her own interests were not at stake, but there is little indication that she possessed any great emotional capacity, though when she gave her affection she gave it in generous measure. In her son there was a gentler streak that can almost be described as sentimental. His emotions were near the surface; when persons of whom he was fond were involved in situations that aroused his sympathy tears came spontaneously to his eyes. There is no record of his mother being similarly moved, sympathetic listener though she often showed herself to be. William was always half man of the world, half dreamer and philosopher, forever asking questions to which he could find no answer. It is natural to ask if this side of his temperament, which was perpetually at war with the more robust qualities displayed by his mother, characterised his father also.

There are difficulties in pursuing this line of inquiry because of the doubts cast by Society on his paternity. Few people within the Lamb circle believed him to be the son of Peniston Lamb, the first Lord Melbourne. Father and son appeared to have little in common. The former has been described as a 'good for little, apathetic, kindly man', who loaded his wife with diamonds on the marriage and was afterwards the rather helpless victim of a rapacious mistress, a man too ineffective to be more than querulous when annoyed or circumvented. There was not even the appearance of much affection between William and his father. The first Viscount's favourite son was his eldest, also a Peniston, a rather more shadowy personality than his younger brothers, and on whose parentage no doubts have been cast. The identity of William's natural father can only be a matter for speculation, if indeed he was not Lord Melbourne's son. His mother managed her private life with the utmost discretion; indeed one of her most bitter complaints against her daughter-in-law, Lady Caroline Lamb, was that she displayed a singular lack of that social virtue. This was an error into which Lady Melbourne herself never fell; she was careful always to behave in public as a well-mannered and dutiful wife. One characteristic of eighteenth-century society was this outward respect for the social conventions; the true relationship between husband and wife or between lover and mistress was veiled in the decent reticence of keeping up appearances.

The general assumption seems to have been that William was the son of Lord Egremont, with whom Lady Melbourne was reputed to have had a semi-permanent relationship. Though later in life Melbourne dismissed the rumour as 'damn nonsense', certainly throughout Egremont's life William was never long without paying him a visit and when the old man felt that his end was drawing near he sent for him. George O'Brien Wyndham was an attractive and intriguing person. He had been born with a golden spoon in his mouth; he was wealthy, good looking and the owner of that magnificent mansion, Petworth House. Like so many eithteenth-century noblemen his interests were wide; he was at once a countryman, a connoisseur and a collector who filled Petworth with *objets d'art* and paintings that gave him pleasure, Claudes, Correggios and Turners. Many, it was said, 'could outshine him in the ballroom, none in the morning ride or garden walk.' Petworth was always filled with guests, artists, men of letters, and political friends; the Wyndhams were a great political family, and through this varied company wandered Lord Egremont, shy, taciturn, eccentric and charming. It was a house William knew well from childhood; Lady Melbourne and her children stayed there frequently. Though she seems to have been no more faithful as a mistress than as a wife - indeed her fourth son George was supposed to have been the result of a brief liaison with the Prince Regent - Lord Egremont appears to have been the man for whom, apart from her sons and William in particular, she felt the deepest and most constant affection.

Whatever the explanation for the mental and emotional conflicts that the adult William had to face, even the most dedicated of modern psychologists could hardly attribute them to a frustrated, affection-starved childhood. Unlike Queen Victoria's, his had been a happy one. The Lamb family were devoted to one another and apart from Peniston, born in 1770 and therefore already a young man of nine when William appeared, they arrived with fair regularity. William was born in

1779, Frederick, the future diplomat, in 1782, George two years later and Emily, the only girl to grow up to womanhood, in 1789. One sister, Harriet, died young. Not many details of their family life survive, but imagination can fill the gap without too much danger of straying far from the actuality. Contemporary accounts depict them as a cheerful, extrovert, somewhat boisterous group of children, given to pranks, to horse play and to loud laughter. At Brocket they had plenty of space in which to work off their high spirits. Though, unlike Petworth, it was not one of the greater 'stately homes', for children it was ideal. There were woods in which to play, a small river where they could fish, and good stabling for their ponies. Like all children of their class they learned to ride early and throughout his life William was a good horseman. Moreover it was a gay house, with people continually coming and going and a sense of bustle and excitement, which William in his Eton days missed with such longing that he was tempted to play truant. Often too the same scenes were repeated at Petworth as friends with their coaches and their horses and servants arrived or departed.

Not all the Lambs' time was spent in the country. Lady Melbourne's role as a political hostess required her presence in London during the season and when Parliament was in session, and the same gaiety permeated Melbourne House in Whitehall, the Melbournes having exchanged their Piccadilly house for that previously owned by the Duke of York in order to oblige His Royal Highness, who had taken a fancy to their original home. As a consequence of the exchange the building which now houses the Scottish Office was William's London home from the time he was ten. It is hardly surprising that he came to take for granted the luxury that surrounded him from childhood, or that he assumed that throughout his life he would mix with the most important personages in Society and in the world of politics. When the Prince of Wales was received by Lady Melbourne on a footing that was, if rumour is to be believed, somewhat more than friendly, so that the children took both him and his rank very much in their stride, William was receiving the kind of training that made him as easy at Court as in the drawing room of any leading hostess. His young life and most impressionable years were lived against a political background and though, unlike the younger Pitt, he never showed any great desire to play an active role in it himself, he grew up knowing instinctively that people were either Whigs or Tories and that politics played a dominating part in the lives of his family and his friends.

Life of course was not all play; children were put to their books early. William was taught to read by his mother's old governess who seems to have been something of a dragon. Though William said his mother adored her, he seems both to have disliked and to have feared her. Writing and the rudiments of Latin were drilled into him by a Mr Cuffage but in spite of his tuition William, as he confessed himself, wrote an ugly hand which late in life became almost illegible. Perhaps he did not concentrate. Like most small boys he was apt to look out of the window and envy the labourers, whom he saw working in the fields at tasks which he thought preferable to mastering this 'confounded Latin'.

At seven he continued his lessons with a local clergyman until he was sent to Eton at the age of nine. It was a bewildering experience for a small boy away from home for the first time. Instead of being supervised by a couple of nursemaids, lest he even got his feet wet, he found himself turned out to play in a field whose banks sloped down to the Thames in which he felt he might well drown. However there were compensations. His father sent him off with ten guineas in his pocket and arranged with a local innkeeper that he be supplied with a further half-a-crown every Monday and Thursday. Not surprisingly the result was that he made himself very sick by eating too many tarts and went home with a spotty face. One of Melbourne's besetting sins throughout his life was an over-indulgence in food.

The Eton to which William went in 1788 differed considerably from modern Eton. The difference between the Collegers, who were on the foundation, and the Oppidans, who paid fees, put its stamp on the entire school, so that Collegers and Oppidans seemed almost like two separate communities divided from each other by social antagonism. For the Colleger life was tough. They lodged together in the notorious Long Chamber where there was unlimited fagging and no check against systematic bullying. Their diet was monotonous, mutton being their staple meat, and the Oppidans, who were given beef, veal, even rabbit on Sundays and mutton never more than twice a week, called their less fortunate school fellows

'Tug-Muttons' or Tugs. The more varied diet of the Oppidans must have been something that William appreciated. Even forty-two years later he still remembered with loathing the boiled mutton and rice pudding that had been his daily nursery fare, voicing his conviction to Victoria that grown-ups first found out what a child most disliked eating and then forced it on their victims every day.

The Oppidans not only ate better, they lodged more comfortably in a Dame's house where they were treated as the sons of gentlemen. Even so the accommodation was spartan after the comforts of Brocket or Melbourne House, particularly for the younger boys. The floors of their rooms were sanded, the windows curtainless and the furniture basic, consisting of a bed, chairs, a table, a desk and a washstand. But their rooms were cleaned for them and unlike the Collegers, who had to eat their breakfast standing in the kitchen or in the discomfort of the yard outside, they could have theirs in comparative comfort. Breakfast for both when William went to Eton consisted of a roll of bread with a pat of butter inside it and either milk or water to drink. William, who disliked milk, drank the latter and later in life spoke scornfully of the practice of drinking tea or coffee or chocolate at breakfast that had crept in since his day. Fagging for Oppidans, as compared with that exacted from junior Collegers, was light. Melbourne himself neither was, nor ever had, a regular fag but the juniors were expected to run errands for the seniors, to field the ball behind the wicket at cricket practice, or find bait for the members of the Fifth and Sixth when they went fishing. Unlike the juniors the seniors had very comfortable studies where fags were expected to toast muffins at tea time or perhaps to brush the coat for some young dandy from the Upper School. Some bullying inevitably went on; small boys were cuffed and beaten and fights were frequent. Later in life Melbourne was to deplore the fact that even at public schools there were too many unpleasant boys who could so easily dominate any youngsters who were physically weak or easily led; looking back he blamed the masters for not interfering more in the fighting that went on. William himself disliked any kind of a rough and tumble tinged with malice, or brutality that so often among boys produced a fight about a trifle. Why get hurt unnecessarily for something quite unimportant? Fights could not always be avoided even by

9

young William but, as he told Victoria later, if he found he was getting the worst of it he gave up and walked away, deterred by no false shame, declaring that it was a silly business. In this the boy was very much the father of the man. Melbourne could always stand on one side, take a detached view, decide the game was not worth the candle and refuse to play. Yet beneath his casual assumption of indifference there was a tougher, more ruthless streak, as later Lord Brougham was to find to his cost. Melbourne once told Victoria that he hoped never to become involved in a duel because he would shoot to kill. Perhaps it was an unconscious awareness of this hidden strength that stopped his school-fellows from dubbing him a coward. In this, as in so much else, he set his own standards and went his own way.

Modern educationalists would consider that the curriculum of Eton was too narrow, based as it was almost entirely on a study of the classics, with other subjects, such as French, only taken as an extra in free time. Even Melbourne, who hated speaking French, was forced to agree that this was unfortunate though, devoted classicist as he was, he disagreed even more firmly with Lord Durham's professed inclination not to have his own son taught Latin. To him it was almost inconceivable that a gentleman could move in Society, where even in Parliament classical tags and allusions adorned so many speeches, without a classical education. It was no accident that Gibbon wrote 'The Decline and Fall' in the eighteenth century. The political world, the literary world, were all steeped in the history and literature of Greece and Rome. Such proficiency was acquired the hard way. Any Eton boy who could not say his assignment received five strokes of the birch. William was lucky in that he had been so well prepared before he went to Eton that the 'confounded Latin' presented him with few difficulties; he was even able to help his less well-equipped friends. Moreover the Under-master, Joseph Goodall, was a sound scholar and inspiring teacher whose lessons William enjoyed. As a result of his earlier proficiency young Lamb was inclined to slack, tempted by all the distractions that Eton had to offer, so that though 'a deuced good scholar' when he went into the Fifth he had become a very bad one by the time he went into the Sixth. Nemesis in the shape of floggings followed. Whatever the psychological effect of physical punishment, in an age that accepted violence and pain as part of the pattern of life, a flogging was something that the young Etonians took very much for granted. It was the usual punishment for bad behaviour and for breaches of the school rules. After the 'Boats' on 4 June, which in Melbourne's time took place without official permission, those participating expected a flogging. When later Queen Victoria argued that the practice was degrading Melbourne did not agree, assuring her that all the boys minded was the pain of it, that he always found that a flogging had an amazing effect on him and that it would have been better if his tutor had flogged him more.

Floggings and fights apart William enjoyed Eton, its companionship, its scholarship, its freedom and its traditions. It was at Eton that he had his first introduction to power; never, he declared, did he feel so 'lowered' as when he came home after lording it as a senior, an experience he must have shared with many a prefect since. All his life the chimes of a great clock reminded him of the school clock by which his days had been regulated and so used had he become to relying on its sound that he never brought himself to wear a watch, relying on some internal clock or calling out to a servant to ask the time. 'Forty Year on, in the dim distance golden' he had indeed 'forgotten the tears' as nostalgically he described his school days to the young Victoria.

Cambridge, where in 1796 he was entered at Trinity College, proved something of an anti-climax. The university was still in the process of freeing itself from medieval clerical traditions. Only a poor scholar who aimed at a fellowship, a tutorship with some noble family or a career in the Church was expected to attend lectures and proceed to a degree. Young men of Lamb's position put in a few terms to round off their education between school and the Grand Tour. Noblemen even wore different gowns to distinguish them from the common herd. They were free to pass their time as they pleased, riding, shooting, gaming, drinking and wenching, with study as a kind of vague and undemanding background. Lacking academic discipline it was easy to do very little serious reading. Nevertheless, because the majority of them came from homes where their families had collected pictures and built up libraries and were no mere fox-hunting, port-swilling squires, they devoted at least some of their time to improving their minds. Though looking back Lamb felt that the two years he spent at Cambridge were largely wasted owing to his own lack of application, he seems to have

11

done a good deal of rather casual reading which embraced anything from his beloved classics through theology to Shakespeare, though he never showed any interest in mathematics. The one positive achievement to his credit during his time at Cambridge was to win the university prize for a set oration on 'The Progressive Improvement of Mankind'. It was an odd mixture, within the conventional framework, of the idealistic streak that often pervaded his early thinking and of the cautious detached views that were later so characteristic of him.

In 1799, when Lamb came down from Cambridge, the war between Britain and France was approaching a climax which meant that the traditional Grand Tour, even for Whigs who sympathised with revolutionary France, was an impracticable way of completing their education. A possible alternative was to attend one of the Scottish universities. In Scotland this was the age of the Enlightenment. Unhampered by the imposition of religious tests, which in England prevented any but members of the Established Church from taking a degree, so excluding many brilliant scholars, Scotland since the time of Adam Smith was attracting some of the best minds of the day and the reputation of its universities was high. Two old family friends of the Melbournes, the Duke of Bedford and Lord Lauderdale, therefore suggested that William and his younger brother Frederick might round off their education by spending some time at Glasgow. William rather liked the idea and arrangements were made for the two young men to board with Professor Miller, who, as was customary, took a few selected students into his own house. Harry Temple, the future Lord Palmerston, who was to be a brilliant politician and a colleague of William's, went to the rival university of Edinburgh in 1800.

Glasgow was a great contrast in every way both to Cambridge, with its lounging ways, and to the luxury of Melbourne House and Brocket. Frederick wrote to his mother 'There is nothing heard of in this house but study' though later he reported that his brother was bombarding the Misses Miller with poetry, without much apparent success. Except at the weekends the daily routine was rigorous. The students in the house were rarely out of it or the lecture rooms, where all the instruction was given in Latin, for more than an hour and even after the evening meal, which usually finished about eleven, they were expected to put in a further session of reading until nearly two. The only concession to sloth was a half-past-nine breakfast and then Frederick complained that an enthusiastic student of mathematics roused him by eight. In contrast the week-ends were given up to social life of a slightly provincial kind. Describing these activities William told his mother 'We drink healths at dinner, hand round the cake at tea, and put our spoons into our cups when we desire to have no more.' One local custom which he thought 'a devilish good one, which ought to be adopted everywhere' was the practice after the cheese of handing round the table 'a bottle of whiskey and another of brandy, and the whole company, male and female, in general indulge in a dram. This is very comfortable and very exhilarating and affords an opportunity for many jokes'. Such parties must have been a very pleasant break in the disciplined life that both young men were now leading and it is easy to picture William's enjoyment as his loud laugh rang out in response to some witticism or when one of his own more extravagant assertions provoked the company to argument. He was as much at ease in Glasgow as in London and Lord Minto, with whom he had dined, described him as 'a remarkably pleasant, clever and well informed young man' – a verdict that London society was to echo.

If William accepted and enjoyed such social opportunities as Glasgow had to offer, he was more critical of his fellow students and thought that over-concentration on academic pursuits was 'very much calculated to make a man vain, important and pedantic' quoting as an example a fellow lodger at Miller's 'who knew nothing before he came here last year, and who therefore thinks that nobody knows anything anywhere else.' Though he was stimulated by and interested in Miller's philosophical theories, he did not allow himself to become completely absorbed by his academic studies and wrote verse as a diversion. This did not necessarily indicate a poetic disposition; one result of a classical education was that men who from boyhood had been subjected to the cadence of classical prose and verse found little difficulty in expressing themselves through this medium. William was no exception, though he told his mother that in his opinion 'prose writing requires as correct an ear as poetry, for it is certainly more various.' Some of the poems which he sent to her from Glasgow apparently met with a cool reception because he wrote back complaining that 'you do not seem to give me any credit for novelty of thought' Many of his letters to her were concerned with the political situation. As a good Whig he was so violently pro-French that in the January of 1800 he was trembling for France and wishing 'the French may be able to defend themselves from their enemies at home and abroad!' He declared bitterly: 'We are fixed in bigotry and prejudice. We think there is no liberty but our liberty, no government but our government, and no religion but our religion.' In this instance the views of the student were no father to those of the future prime minister but William's vehemence was not without influence on his future life. According to her own confession Lady Caroline Lamb 'fell in love when only twelve years old with a friend of Charles James Fox – a friend of liberty, whose poems I had read, whose self I had never seen', and when finally they met it was William's daring opinions, 'his love of liberty and independence' as much as his good looks that made thirteen-year-old Caroline 'adore him'.

Glasgow, unlike Eton, had been an interlude in his life rather than a moulding factor. It had been pleasant enough in a way and had enriched his store of philosophical thought but even the two years that he had spent there had been interrupted by vacations, when he had returned to the fashionable distractions of London. In consequence he had never been subjected for more than a few months at a time to the discipline of constant application even to subjects in which his interest was keen and genuine. Bouts of academic involvement interspersed with bouts of relaxing, sauntering pleasure were not sufficient to inculcate in him those habits of steady application of which, later, on some occasions of his public life, he was to show himself capable. When he returned to London with his studies complete and was faced with the necessity of adopting some settled career and habits of life, it was as a young man of many and diverse interests who nevertheless still lacked the dedication to any aim or cause or ambition that could give a sense of direction and purpose to his future.

2

EARLY MANHOOD

WILLIAM LAMB was now twenty-one. His life had been singularly fortunate as the world counts fortune, though had his early years been less unclouded his personality might have struck deeper roots instead of reaching to the sun. His childhood had been happy, he had enjoyed Eton, Cambridge had presented very little challenge and imposed no visible strains. Even Glasgow had only added a few more sober tints to the background of his life provided by fashionable Society and the splendid leisure of the great country houses where the Melbournes were always welcome guests. His mother's expertise had opened to her favourite son the entrance to this exclusive world; his own good looks, high spirits and charm had made him welcome there. He was soon able to count some of the most famous London hostesses as his friends, including the formidable Lady Holland and the beautiful Duchess of Devonshire. Women liked William Lamb and in turn he found female society a necessity to him. Like most young men of his age and class no doubt he considered sexual adventures a normal part of a bachelor's existence, but, like his mother, he was discreet over his affairs. Opportunities certainly were not lacking, either among the married woman of his acquaintance or among the demi-monde, the world of Harriet Wilson and her like. But what he valued most, one may hazard an opinion, was an easy relationship with women who were well bred, charming and intelligent. Unlike George Canning, whose career in some ways provides an interesting parallel to his own, wide though the differences in their parentage and childhood had been, William seems to have made few close and intimate friends of his own age, either at Eton or at Cambridge. Perhaps he was at once too popular and too self reliant to need the kind of reassurance that such relationships imply. On the one hand he never felt the lack of friends: they came too easily. On the other the blank spaces between his many social activities could be, and were, filled by his love of reading, which gave him many hours of tranquil pleasure. Probably this is only half the explanation. The Lambs were a singularly united and devoted family. They always had been since the days when Lady Melbourne had trailed her lively brood round with her between Melbourne House, Brocket and Petworth. While William had his brothers Fred and George with whom to joke, to devise practical pranks and to indulge in the amateur theatricals which provided one of their most absorbing pastimes, he had no need of other close companions. Moreover there was always his mother in the background to listen and to advise. With both sides of his nature, the social and the reflective, provided for so adequately he was well equipped to enjoy to the full all that fortune offered.

Yet, like many young men passing from adolescence into early manhood, William Lamb had his moods of nostalgic meloncholy, bemoaning the lost innocence of youth and assuming a pose of mature cynicism. For such moods verse has always provided a congenial means of expression, and William was no exception, churning out such lines as:

> Well it is if, when dawning manhood smiled
> We did not quite forget the simple child;
> If, when we lost that name we did not part
> From some more glowing virtue of the heart.'

The virtues he listed were 'kind benevolence', 'the generous candour of believing youth' and 'the soft spirit which men weakness call,' all were qualities for which he believed 'the cold endownments of the head' to be but a poor exchange. It is not easy to determine whether such sentiments marked more than a passing mood and should be taken as indication that already he was departing from the frothy idealism of his Cambridge oration, with its belief that the progressive improvement of mankind was possible, and his dedication to the cause of revolutionary France. There must be few who, having crossed the threshold of adult life, do not suffer from some degree of disillusion when they experience the difference between the dream and reality, though their dreams may not have been those professed by William, 'painted pleasures' charms, Wine's liberal powers, and beauty's folding arms'. Many students, whose goal has long been the university, experience the same sense of anti-climax during their first year. Moreover when William indulged in such reflections he was only expressing sentiments that were fashionable. This was the period of the Romantic poets, when men of sentiment were almost expected to be conscious of their garments of immortality and when the innocence of youth was a cliché. It is difficult to believe that after the rough and tumble of Eton, the years at Cambridge and Glasgow, and his experience of fashionable society, a society over which the Regent and his old schoolfellow Beau Brummel presided, a young man as intelligent as William Lamb would not have had his eyes opened to the follies and insincerities of the world around him, particularly when he had a mother as worldly-wise and sophisticated as Lady Melbourne. Nevertheless, artificial as his verses seem, they may well have been an expression of his realisation that one phase of his life was over and that both its pleasures and its pains were something which he would never again experience in quite the same way.

His immediate problem was to decide on a future career. As a younger son he was expected to make his own way in the world, helped no doubt by whatever influence his family or his friends might exert on his behalf. It is perhaps slightly surprising that Lady Melbourne failed to persuade one of her many friends to use their patronage to find him some well-paid, undemanding post. There were four other main choices open to any young man in William's position, the Army, the Navy, the Church and the Law. In the seventeenth and early eighteenth centuries it had not been unusual for gentlemen's sons to be apprenticed to prominent London merchants trading overseas, but even had such a career still been acceptable it is difficult to imagine young Lamb dealing with ledgers and bills of lading. In the twentieth century he might have become a popular actor, enthusiastic as all the Lambs were about amateur theatricals, but, whatever his talents in that direction, at the beginning of the nineteenth this would have been unthinkable. Neither the Army nor the Navy attracted him. He hated the mere thought of death and anything connected with it, and shrank from the sordid, the harsh and cruel. Moreover in 1800 there was another difficulty. Both would have involved fighting against the French and William's sympathies were still with France. His choice therefore lay between the Church and the Law. Despite his interest in theology he was not much drawn to the former, though he would have made an impressive and even learned bishop. Only the law remained. Canning, also, as a young man who lacked the means to go into Parliament, had opted for the Law as a career, but his attitude towards it was very different from that adopted by William. Canning accepted the fact that the way to success would be long, rugged and toilsome but this was something that he thought well worth while so long as at the end of the road lay independence and power. There is nothing to suggest that William shared the sentiments of his future political chief. Unlike Canning, an actress's son, the good things of life had come to William too easily and he had no inclination to work hard or endure the drudgery inseparable from success in the legal profession.

Unfanned by the winds of ambition William, who had joined the Northern circuit, was launched on his legal career by a brief from a friendly solicitor, for which he earned a guinea. The prospect of further briefs seemed bleak. Progress at the Bar is notoriously slow but he did not seem unduly worried; he found the life a pleasant one and his fellow barristers good company. Even had he applied himself to the furtherance of his professional prospects with all the energy and devotion that Canning thought so essential, it is questionable whether William, in spite of his melodious voice and clear mind, was the stuff of which good barristers are made. He was too prone to see both sides of any question and too unable to commit himself to either with the partisanship needed to make a good advocate. Though he was admitted to the Bar as a Special Pleader in 1804 he seems to have spent more time at Holland House, where since 1799 he had been a welcome guest, at Devonshire House and at the Melbourne's own town house, than in his chambers at

4 Pump Court. Apart from these social activities he was more interested in writing verse than in mastering briefs; he continued to saunter through life.

What the future would have held when this pleasant but apparently purposeless pattern began to pall can never be known because it was brought to an abrupt end by the death of his eldest brother Peniston in January 1805, probably of consumption. When Lady Bessborough, William's future mother-in-law visited the Melbournes to provide what comfort she could, the whole family was in a state of deep distress. Lady Melbourne was almost inconsolable at the death of her first born; whatever other criticisms could be brought against her she had always shown herself to be a devoted mother. To Lord Melbourne it must have been a particularly shattering blow. Peniston was definitely his own son; of none of the other children could he feel so certain. William was now his heir; was he also his son? The fact that he would eventually succeed to the title and estates transformed William's life. Eldest sons as a matter of course went into the House of Commons, where they served their political apprenticeship before proceeding to the Lords on their father's death, and Lord Melbourne had been engaged before Peniston had died in the necessary negotiations for his election. He had also signified his intention to make him an allowance of £5,000 a year. For William he was prepared to do less, and while recognising that a seat in the Commons must be found for him, he refused to allow him more than £2,000 a year. Even so this represented a new independence. There was little difficulty in finding a seat and in January 1806 he was elected member for Leominster. His new career had begun.

At first it seemed as if his customary good fortune was about to attend him because after a long time in the political wilderness his friends were in power. The connection between the Melbournes and the Hollands was close and in 1806 Charles James Fox, the leading light of the group and Lord Holland's uncle, was Secretary of State in Lord Grenville's ministry. When William Lamb started his apprenticeship the party system in its modern form was beginning to crystallise out of a still fluid situation. This continuous process was to form the background of Melbourne's political career, first as Home Secretary and then as Prime Minister. The two traditional party names, Whig and Tory, go back to the Exclusion campaign of

1679 but over the century party views had undergone many a sea change as each manoeuvred for position in changing political circumstances. In the mid-eighteenth century it had almost seemed as if a two-party system would not continue to dominate politics. The fierce strife of Anne's reign, as each party struggled to secure the throne on her death for its own candidate, ended in a Whig victory which threatened to destroy the Tories as a political fighting force. By the middle of the century Britain had become in practice, though not in theory, a one-party state controlled by the Whigs. This did not put an end to political intrigue and in-fighting on the part of ambitious politicians; the fighting was now between groups within the party, each gathered round some prominent leader, each fighting for office rather than for policy. This was the heyday of aristocratic government in Britain, the Whigs representing the wealth of the great landowners with, as useful allies, the financial and commercial interests. The Bank of England was itself a Whig creation. Active, ambitious politicians all called themselves Whigs, leaving the label Tory to the largely independent and almost non-political country gentlemen, who shared a common outlook rather than thought of themselves as a party. With the American War of Independence the situation changed again. Since the accession of George III in 1760 the great Whig party had fractured into two opposing groups, one enjoying the favour of the Crown, the other struggling to regain it. After 1776 political strife was given a new validity because once again there were very genuine differences of opinion as to how the American revolt should be handled. Out of this conflict, which culminated in the recognition of American independence, a new Tory party began to emerge, led after 1783 by the younger Pitt, though he and his followers continued to think of themselves as government Whigs. Nevertheless by the turn of the century when contemporeries spoke of 'the Whigs' they were referring to that coalition of wealthy aristocratic families whose political leader was Charles James Fox.

Both Lord and Lady Holland were to play an important part in Melbourne's personal and political life. He was a singularly sweet-tempered person, she a more forceful one. Their marriage had been a love match. Lady Holland, the daughter of a wealthy West Indian planter, had been married previously to Sir Godfrey Webster before eloping with Henry Richard Fox.

Their first son Charles had been born out of wedlock, but after a divorce had been secured in 1797 the couple had been able to marry. When Lady Bessborough saw them the same day she was enchanted by their happiness and devotion to one another, a devotion which continued throughout their life. The stricter elements in London society were less approving. Though this same society was riddled with adultery, amours were discreet and broken marriages few, possibly because a divorce required a private act of Parliament and possibly even more because in a society where land was the base of family prestige the material repercussions of a divorce might be inconvenient. So, for most people, the marriage vow was stretched, not broken, and proved itself sufficiently elastic to accommodate most emotional situations. Though some people refused to recognise Lady Holland, who was not received at Court, a circumstance which Melbourne once told Queen Victoria was a source of severe mortification to her, this did not prevent Holland House, their magnificent home, from being a magnet which attracted not only the wealthy and well born but also the most interesting and intelligent people in town. Lady Holland was a masterful hostess who made her own rules and expected her guests, however eminent, to observe them, though on one occasion later in life Melbourne, as he then was, on being ordered to change his seat at the dining table, declared with his customary verbal vigour that he would be 'damned' if he dined with her at all and stamped out of the room. By then he was a privileged old friend. Lady Holland expected her privileges too and when he was prime minister he tried to avoid the famous red boxes being brought to him at Holland House as its mistress seemed to think she had the right to know their contents.

Another famous Whig hostess was Georgiana, Duchess of Devonshire. She also was an ardent supporter of Charles James Fox. It is said that she bribed a butcher to vote for Fox, in the vital election of 1784, by bestowing on him a kiss in public. The lovely duchess was never a stickler for proprieties and life at Devonshire House, as later described by Lady Caroline, was an almost hilarious mixture of grandeur and utter disorganisation. At Holland House an uninvited guest, even an old friend, would be refused admittance; at Devonshire House it could be doubted if either the Duchess or her staff knew with any certainty who had been invited and who had not. But in the social hierarchy the most important Whig house was Carlton House, the residence of George, Prince of Wales. The day had not yet come when it was considered unconstitutional for the Crown to have known political views; on the contrary it was almost traditional for politicians out of favour with the Court to attach themselves to the Prince of Wales, hoping that when he became King he would reward their devotion, an optimism apparently unhampered by the historical fact that he very rarely did. The gulf between the elderly George III and his heir was of long standing and was complicated by clashing personalities as well as by political friction. In this clash Charles James Fox, and therefore all the Holland clan, was involved with important repercussions on Britain's political history. George III had disliked Charles James's father, the first Lord Holland, an able but unscrupulous politician, and that dislike had been intensified by the character of his son. Contemporaries bore vivid testimony to his charm, wit and intelligence, but the younger Fox was a compulsive gambler, whose personal life was irregular and who, in George III's eyes, exercised a disastrous influence over the Prince of Wales. For the short periods in which Fox held high office he seemed able to slough off his disreputable ways and to prove both that he could apply himself to business and that he had very considerable abilities. Perhaps unfortunately both for the country and for himself the periods in which he could exercise these abilities were short. During the American War of Independence he had championed the cause of the rebel colonists in the Commons; it was during his brief tenure of power that the Treaty of Versailles recognised them as a sovereign power. It was because Fox knew that the King would never willingly give him office that he had cultivated the Prince of Wales, who was at that time a young man on the verge of his majority. To the dismay of his father the young Prince and the older politician became boon companions. By 1806 he was no longer a Prince Charming but a middle aged roué with a spreading figure. Nevertheless he was the hope of the Whigs. George III was subject to a rare disease, porphyria, the symptoms of which during a severe attack resembled those usually associated with insanity. In addition he was aging rapidly. There had been talk of a Regency before but with the political cards stacked against them it seemed unlikely that the Whigs would ever be asked to form a government while power remained with the old King. Then in January 1806, the same month that William Lamb was returned for Leominster, William Pitt died. Lord Grenville who, though one of the Whig stalwarts, had broken with Fox and Sheridan in 1793 over their support for France and had joined Pitt's government, was the man whom George III was forced, for lack of a man he liked better, to ask to form the new administration. Grenville took the Treasury himself and Fox went to the Foreign Office. At last the stage seemed set for a Whig government.

Thus it happened that William Lamb began his political career under what seemed the most favourable of auspices, with influential friends prepared to push his interests. Unlike Canning, William had not chosen politics but rather had been chosen by politics and it is fascinating to speculate to what extent at this time his political views were the result of his Whig environment and the influence of Fox and Sheridan. The problem is more intriguing because the views that he had expressed on such matters before his entry into Parliament contrast so markedly with those that he held as Home Secretary, and later as Prime Minister. At the beginning of his public life he was an ardent Foxite. In this too the parallel between himself and Canning is interesting. Both young men as students had expressed emotional sympathy with the French Revolution, but Canning, the elder of the two, had found himself increasingly drawn to Pitt, had entered Parliament as his protégé, and had taken up an anti-French position. It was Canning who had been one of the moving spirits behind the propaganda publication *The Anti-Jacobin*, published in 1798. It was amusing, witty, full of sparkling topical verse, the kind of exercise in which Canning with his trenchant pen excelled. By this time he no longer counted himself a Whig; he was a Pittite and possibly one of his best remembered sallies, published in *The Anti-Jacobin*, was the lines describing a Whig as

> A steady patriot of the World alone,
> The friend of every country- - -but his own.

while he claimed that the mission of *The Anti-Jacobin* was

> From mental mists to purge the Nation's eyes,
> To animate the weak, unite the wise.

and finally

> To drive and scatter all the brood of Lies,
> And chase the flying Falsehood as it flies;
> The long arrears of Ridicule to pay,
> And drag reluctant Dulness back to day.

Smarting under Canning's attack the Whigs rallied their own versifiers to reply and in the Morning Chronicle William retaliated with the lines,

> Hail justly famous who with fancy blest,
> Use fiend-like Virulance for sportive Jest
> Who only bark to serve your private ends--
> Patrons of Prejudice, Corruption's friends!
> Who hurl your venomed darts at well earned fame,
> Virtue you hate and Calumny your aim.

going on to castigate 'youthful C---g with powers mechanical far above his age' despite the fact that the latter was in truth nine years William's senior.

The fact that his friends were in office brought the new member into the limelight early. On 29 December 1806 he was chosen to move the address in reply to the Speech from the Throne, which enabled him to break the parliamentary ice and deliver his maiden speech on a set occasion instead of having either to choose a topic or make an opportunity to intervene in a debate. Speechifying did not come easily to him. At the dinner table when the conversation and wine flowed freely he could delight his companions with his caustic comments, his verbal extravagances and what he called 'the sportive jest', with engaging ease, but to intervene in a debate was something from which he shrank. Later in the session, when the Solicitor General introduced a bill to make the freehold estates of persons dying insolvent assets for the payment of simple contract debts, a proposal which Lamb thought equitable but which the country gentlemen regarded as an attack on landed property and were therefore determined to defeat, his nerve failed him, as the entry in his briefly kept journal shows. 'I entered the House', he wrote, 'with the fullest intention of speaking and, as I thought, having sufficiently considered the subject. Many excellent opportunities offered themselves, but my resolution always failed me, which I have bitterly regretted ever since.' It is a revealing confession which helps to explain the very inactive part he played in Commons debates. It was not merely the distractions of society, nor absorption in his private problems in the early years of his political apprenticeship, though both no doubt helped to distract him, so much as an inability to thrust himself into the fray, even when, as on this occasion, his failure to do so 'really hurt and mortified me deeply'. Even Lady Bessborough, now his mother-in-law, anxious as she was to praise him, had to admit to Glanville Leveson Gower that he could not really be considered a first-class speaker. Inhibited as he was it is not surprising to find that his speeches were few and far between. In any case whatever advantage might have accrued to him from the friendship of the leading Whigs soon disappeared. Fox's death in September 1806 left the ministry without a common leader to whom all the various sections of the party could look up, and though when Lord Grenville decided to hold an election the Whigs appeared to have increased their majority, Lamb had joined a ship already beginning to founder in the political sea.

The reason why it sank played little part in Lamb's political career. Basically the Whigs were divided into three groups, the followers of Grenville, who represented the old Whig tradition, the followers of Fox, who advocated the abolition of the Slave Trade and who still had some remnants of his original commitment to parliamentary reform, and finally a rather more radical group of younger men, critical of contemporary institutions and methods of thinking. To keep all these three in any sort of alignment was beyond Grenville's capability but the Slave Trade at least was abolished. The rock on which the government eventually foundered was the vexed question of Ireland and Roman Catholic Emancipation. This was a hang-over from earlier fears of popish domination that stretched back to memories of the Spanish Armada, intensified by the knowledge that a discontented Roman Catholic Ireland would provide the national enemy, France, with an ideal base from which to launch an invasion of England. Partly in order to gain direct control of Ireland an Act of Union had been forced through the English and Irish parliaments in 1801, but prejudice and fear had prevented the taking of the only steps which would have made the sacrifice of Irish institutions acceptable to them, namely the placing of Roman Catholics on an equal footing with Protestants in the matter of promotion within the services and the right to send co-religionists to represent them in the united Parliament at Westminster. Public opinion in England, as demonstrated by the Gordon Riots that led to the pillaging and burning of London as late as 1780, and shared by George III, made this solution politically impossible. The result was a trickle of half measures. For example Roman Catholics were allowed to vote for their representatives at Westminster, but these had to be Protestants; no Roman Catholic could sit in the House of Commons. Similar limitations affected the Army. Roman Catholics were only allowed to hold commissions up to the rank of colonel; above that they were considered to be politically dangerous; moreover even this concession only applied to Irish troops in Ireland. Grenville's ministry was anxious to win support both in Ireland and among its own party by removing these restrictions and also throwing open staff appointments to Roman Catholics, a measure for which there were good practical reasons in time of war. This was political dynamite and ministers soon realised that they could not carry the measure in face of the resistance of the Tory opposition, combined with George III's conviction that to sign such a bill would contravene his coronation oath. Consequently they decided to drop the measure. When however the King demanded that in addition they should pledge themselves never to raise the issue of Roman Catholic Emancipation again, they felt themselves unable to accept such a condition and the ministry fell.

As Lamb was not an office holder this only affected his parliamentary career in so far as, with the rest of his friends, he now went into Opposition. Apparently he shared their views as he seconded the motion to the effect that ministers cannot bind themselves by pledges that would limit their future policy in any way, a view to which he adhered consistently throughout his political career. But the speech in which he argued his point made no obvious impact on the House and the impression left by his contemporaries is that it was very much in the nature of a set piece with very little spontaneity behind it. In any case it was defeated by 258 votes to 226. For the next few years Lamb was at least as much preoccupied by his social life and personal problems as with his official career. He spoke only on such topics as interested him and he did not always follow the party line. Indeed he was becoming increasingly disenchanted with Whig politics and increasingly inclined to support the ministry in its prosecution of the war. He was certainly not 'a friend of every country but his own' any longer and he was beginning to see in his old adversary Canning a man with whose politics he had much sympathy. Canning meanwhile at the age of thirty-five had achieved his ambition; he was Foreign Secretary in the new Tory administration while his close friend Lord Liverpool went to the Home Office. Unfortunately for the harmony of the Portland administration Canning and Castlereagh, the Secretary of War, could not work together and in September 1809 their mutual distrust flared into a duel which forced them both to resign. When the Duke of Portland died in October the shattered ministry was reformed under Spencer Perceval who remained at the Treasury until his assassination in 1812, the only British prime minister to be removed from his office in this way. These changes in the ministry might have afforded Lamb an opportunity of joining the government, as apparently Portland did approach him before his death with an offer which he declined. His reasons for this, he told Lady Bessborough, were in the first place that he was unwilling to tie himself by accepting a place in an administration that was made up of so many discordant persons and secondly that, though on most occasions he was prepared to support the government with his vote, he knew that many things would be brought forward which he would dislike and therefore he was determined to remain unpledged.

During Perceval's administration William Lamb continued to take a fairly independent line, supporting the Government's war effort but voting with the Whig opposition on the matter of the involvement of the Duke of York in his mistress's, Mrs Anne Clarke's, management of army promotions for cash, and generally supporting the Whigs in their attack on political corruption. For instance in 1810 he spoke in favour of a bill promoted by an MP called Fuller to abolish sinecure posts. His speech was one full of shrewd political reasoning in which he argued that men holding such posts could never be genuinely independent while men disappointed in their expectation of a sinecure were likely to go into factious opposition, which was something of which he always disapproved. Though in opposition himself at the time of speaking, Lamb made a clear mental distinction between opposing government measures merely to embarrass the ministry and opposing them because he disapproved of them. The first line was taken in general by his Whig friends, the second was that adopted as his own rule of conduct. It was not an attitude to commend itself to a party struggling in the wilderness and Lady Bessborough admitted that most people would regard such conduct as over-scrupulous and conscientious for a good party man, though personally she admired his firm integrity. His attitude to factious opposition was that subscribed to, at least in theory, by eighteenth-century politicians, namely that it was the duty of members of both Houses to support the King's ministers unless the advice they tendered to him was clearly endangering the national interest. Such a doctrine was capable of a very wide interpretation and there was in practice plenty of factious opposition in the eighteenth century as politicians manoeuvred for place and power. Even William Lamb, as a young man writing to his mother from Glasgow, was prepared to concede that in public relations an opposition had a psychological benefit. 'While there is an Opposition in the House of Commons' he wrote, 'people think that their rights are taken care of, and go to sleep. When there is none they feel themselves more in the hands of Ministry (not that they really are so) and begin to watch for themselves.' In the day-to-day business of politics William was hampered by his own intellectual honesty; for party purposes he could never bring himself to see black as white, or for that matter white as black; the best he could achieve was to distinguish between various shades of grey. Moreover he was too clear-sighted to believe the passionate arguments put forward by either side. Essentially he was a middle-of-the-road man, a quality that was to stand him in good stead where as prime minister he had to keep a difficult team together, but one that was unlikely to accelerate his progress to office. Meanwhile he continued to go his own way, now voting with the Government, now supporting one of the more radical members of his own party, Sir Samuel Romilly, in his attempts to mitigate the brutal penal code which made the theft of property valued at five shillings a capital offence.

After the Whigs had been three years in opposition, a recurrence of George III's old malady late in 1810 made it look as if a Regent would have to be appointed. This could only be the Prince of Wales and the Whigs were confident, over-confident as it proved, that he would use his new authority to dismiss his Tory ministers and call his friends to power. Therefore the form which the Regency bill, introduced by Perceval into the Commons in December, would take appeared to them as of paramount importance. Perceval shared this view and, like the younger Pitt faced with a very similar situation in 1788, was anxious to limit the Regent's powers. To such limitations the Whigs were equally naturally opposed. In the subsequent debates William supported his friends, arguing that it was dangerous to tie the hands of the executive in time of war, and that to do so in this particular case was to show an unjustified distrust of the Prince himself. How far was this Whig special pleading, how far William's own opinion? Certainly he was in a position to speak about His Royal Highness from personal knowledge, having been in and out of Carlton House since boyhood. Certainly too he was in favour of a strong executive in time of war, a war that at that moment was going far from well. It is sometimes forgotten that all Lamb's political thinking was done against a background of a war that, except for the brief interlude of the Peace of Amiens, had dragged on for seventeen years, bringing with it all the by-products of inflation, dear food and spasmodic bouts of trade depression. However justified the arguments of the Whigs might have been the Government was strong enough to impose the restrictions that it thought desirable for a period of twelve months, arguing that should the King recover within that time it would be awkward if the Prince Regent had been free to make drastic changes of which his father would not have approved. Even so the Regent's Whig friends expected some immediate signs of his favour and waited hopefully for the news of Perceval's dismissal, particularly as they were well aware that personally the Regent did not like him. Hope was soon deferred, though not immediately abandoned. Then in January it appeared as if the King might make a speedy recovery. This gave the Regent, who was himself well aware of the difficulties of swapping horses in mid-stream, the excuse for making no changes in his ministry. The hopes of a royal recovery soon faded, and by December 1811 the restrictions on the Regent's powers expired. This left him in an awkward position *vis à vis* his friends. Even though he had no great liking for Perceval and his colleagues he approved of their general policy. Moreover he was suspicious of what his Whig friends, given their heads, might do. During their years in Opposition they had attacked 'corruption' or in other words many of the methods used by the executive to maintain a reliable parliamentary majority. Moreover they had espoused the cause of Roman Catholic Emancipation which the Prince was shrewd enough to realize would stir up a hornets' nest at a time when all government attention ought to be concentrated on resisting Napoleon. Yet he felt himself bound to make some gesture to them. Accordingly he offered them some places in the ministry without inviting them to form a new and completely Whig administration. To have accepted would therefore have meant accepting policies of which they did not approve and have hamstrung any attempts to introduce those more radical ones for which they had been campaigning while in opposition. Therefore they refused, leaving the Tories in sole control. William Lamb himself again apparently received an offer of office which the Regent personally pressed him to accept, arguing shrewdly enough that to refuse now would jeopardise his future chances because the leading Whig politicians were at once too negligent and too arrogant to bring forward the younger menbers of the party. Lamb, however, decided to stay with his friends, though he continued to disagree with the more extreme members of the now disgruntled opposition, and when on Perceval's death the ministry was reconstructed under Lord Liverpool, Lamb decided not to stand for re-election to the new Parliament.

His reasons for this decision seem to have been more personal than political. Since 1806 he had not only been an MP; he had also been a married man and his marriage had proved itself as stormy and incident-crammed as his parliamentary life had been smooth and uneventful. Moreover an income that was adequate for a bachelor was not sufficient to keep an extravagent wife. So, reluctantly, if his letter to his mother can be taken at its face value, William decided that he could not afford the expenses of an election campaign, which was an extremely costly business in pre-reform days. Politics and the House of Commons, in spite of a considerable degree of disillusion with Whig policies, had become his way of life and he acknowledged that he would miss being a member. Also, as he stressed in outlining the position to his mother, it was now late for him to turn to another career and hitherto politics had been the great object of his life. How far these protestations were completely genuine it is difficult to judge. William knew how ambitious his mother was for him and he may have overstressed his own disappointment in having to give up a political career when he said it was tantamount to cutting his own throat. But in any case he had little alternative, or at least he felt this to be the case, though Lady Melbourne told Lord Holland that his contention that he could not afford to stand was nonsense. The stark fact was that Lord Melbourne was not prepared to make the necessary funds available and this was decisive. Between 1812 and 1816, when he was offered a seat at Northampton, he was out of Parliament; his political career had apparently come to an end. By the time he succeeded to the title and took his place in the Lords it could have been too late.

3

LADY CAROLINE'S HUSBAND

EVEN before William Lamb had become a Member of Parliament he had already taken a step that was to influence him profoundly and to colour the rest of his life. On 3 June 1805 he married Lady Caroline Ponsonby, Lady Bessborough's daughter. She had only been a child of thirteen, though a precocious thirteen, when he had first met her and for the last four years he had been deeply in love with her, a fact which he had kept to himself. Marriages in the eighteenth century were not normally arranged on a basis of mutual attraction. They were a matter for the two families involved, and love, though desirable – indeed no affectionate and considerate parent would force a daughter to marry a man she actively disliked – was not the main requisite. Aristocratic society, for all its glitter and elegance, was fundamentally based on property and especially on property in land. Marriages were the prime method of enlarging an estate and increasing the consequence of a family. Emotions came and went; land remained. A man must at least be able to maintain a wife in the style to which she was accustomed before any parent would consent to marriage. Such marriages were not necessarily between persons of equal social status. The heir to an encumbered estate might marry a rich merchant's daughter; he got money, she acquired rank and the entry into a society in which she had not been born. In the same way a daughter might marry beneath her if her aristocratic father could not afford to give her a substantial dowry. A younger son had either to make a fortune, acquire a competency, or marry money, and this again usually entailed exchanging birth for money. Love alone was no reason for matrimony. These were the accepted canons of society and William Lamb knew that his nebulous prospects at the Bar, and his own not inexpensive tastes, meant that he could not possibly be considered by Lord and Lady Bessborough as a suitable match for Caroline. So, since honour forbade him declaring himself, young Lamb did his best to overcome his feelings by the time-honoured means of keeping out of her way and trying to fix his affections elsewhere, probably outside the confines of matrimony, and by filling his life with other interests. In this he was unsuccessful. His love for Caroline remained unshaken and as soon as Peniston's death made him the heir to the title and estates he began his courtship.

The attraction between them was mutual. Even before he had thought of her as more than an attractive, intelligent thirteen-year-old she had considered herself to be in love with him, a fact which may in itself have made him the more vulnerable to her charms. People might like or dislike Caroline Ponsonby, but they could never ignore her. Her nature was perhaps not so much deep as responsive, like a lovely shallow lake that responds to every wind that agitates its surface and that reflects every change in the sky above, now dancing in the sunshine, now tossing in sudden rage. When she loved she loved deeply with an all-absorbing passion; when she hated the emotion tore her, driving her to extravagant action. Not a great deal is known about her childhood, apart from the anecdotes which later in life she related to her friend, the Irish authoress Lady Morgan. Such material must necessarily always be somewhat suspect; memory has a trick of distorting or highly colouring one's early days and Caroline always had a vivid imagination. According to her own account she was at once a tomboy with a passion for horses and animals and a hyper-sensitive emotional child, adoring her mother, whom she called her 'angel mother', deeply affectionate but quite without self-discipline or self-control. She was certainly not an easy child; all the evidence we have makes that clear. Indeed during adolescence she appeared so emotionally unstable, giving way to terrible bouts of hysteria, that a fashionable physician, Dr

Warren, was called in and asked for his advice. Perhaps on the principle that storms unopposed blow themselves out with the least damage, his advice was that no attempt should be made to restrain her wild moods and that she should not be subjected to the discipline of the school room.

Her instinct, she told Lady Morgan, was for music: 'in it I delighted; I cried when it was pathetic, but I wrote not, I spelt not, but made verses, which they all thought beautiful.' On the other hand she described herself as hating finery, dress and company. Whatever the cause of her highly-strung temperament and capacity for unhappiness, it was certainly not due to the fact that she was an unloved child. However, her background during her young days was an unstable one. Her mother, Lady Duncannon, better known by her later title of Lady Bessborough, was not strong and at first Caroline seems to have spent much of her time with her grandmother, Lady Spencer, and later with her cousins Georginia and Harriet Cavendish and their young brother, the heir to the dukedom, known among the family as Hart. It was not a pattern of living capable of providing a wayward child like Caroline with a tradition of discipline. The children seem to have lived in an atmosphere of magnificent disorder, eating irregular meals served by friendly but casual servants off silver plates and invading the kitchen in search of titbits when ever the fancy moved them. As a result of Dr Warren's advice her education was equally undisciplined and formless; she absorbed only what interested her, with a penchant for the dramatic and the romantic. Much of her information was gleaned from the world around her. Whig society was well-informed and the conversations that she heard ranged from politics and literature to poetry and art. Caroline always loved to shine and she had a quick mind that enabled her to show not only a surprising versatility but also flashes of delighted and delightful insight. As she grew to womanhood her own conversation was full of charm; she was described as 'her voice soft, low, caressing, that was at once a beauty and a charm, and worked much of that fascination that was peculiarly hers; it softened down her enemies the moment they listened to her. She was eloquent, most eloquent, full of ideas, of graceful gracious expression; but her subject was always herself.' Later, when William's courtship was trembling in the balance, Lady Bessborough, summing up

the pros and cons of the marriage to Lord Glanville Leveson
Gower, stressed the fact that William Lamb was very clever,
which quality she thought essential for her daughter's
happiness.

As to whether Lady Caroline was beautiful or not opinions
varied. She was small with a boyish slender figure and she loved
to wear boy's clothes. Her complexion was not particularly
good, though in spite of having the dreaded smallpox at
fourteen she had only two small pock marks on her face. Her
hair was golden, some called it red, and curled all over her head;
her eyes were dark and beautiful. Above all she had that quality
that today we label charisma. Until, later in life, her conduct
became too outrageous, people accepted from her a behaviour,
and at times a brutal frankness of opinion, that in a less
bewitching person they would never have forgiven. As Lady
Morgan averred, 'she confounded her dearest friends and direst
foes, for her feelings were all impulses worked on by a powerful
imagination, all elements of great eloquence, but not good for
guidance; one of her great charms was the rapid transition of
manner which changed to its theme' Above all she genuinely
did not care what people thought of her conduct, partly because
in her own eyes she could do no wrong. She set her own
standards and expected the world to accept them, and even
admire them, because they were hers. Possibly the atmosphere
of Devonshire House was to some extent responsible for her
unconventionality, but the seeds must have lain in her own
temperament. It was this disregard for convention that marked
her out in an age that accepted it as a seemly screen for much
that was promiscuous and adulterous. Her own mother had for
years been the mistress of the charming young Glanville
Leveson Gower, who finally married Lady Bessborough's own
niece, Caroline's nursery companion, Harriet Cavendish. The
beautiful Duchess of Devonshire, Lady Bessborough's sister,
was perhaps even more generous with her favours, while her
husband the Duke divided his between his Duchess and her
closest friend Lady Elizabeth Foster, by whom he had children,
one of whom, another Caroline, married William's brother
George. But what these ladies did with discretion, so that
nobody had to acknowledge what everybody in the swim knew,
Caroline in later life blazoned abroad. It was this trait that so
infuriated her future mother-in-law, Lady Melbourne,

who, though hardly in a position to preach conjugal faithfulness, was certainly entitled to demand from her daughter-in-law that she should observe the decencies imposed by society.

This was the woman whose spell for four years William Lamb had been unable to break, and who now, by the turn of fortune's wheel, was to become his wife. Though the love that bound them was genuine it was a marriage that from the first held seeds of disaster. Lady Bessborough on the eve of the engagement was full of misgivings. As she informed Glanville Leveson Gower it was something which, because of Caroline's early predilection for him, she had always dreaded and tried to prevent. She had never wanted William to offer for her daughter. Though ostensibly a friend of Lady Melbourne's she did not really like the connection. Moreover she disapproved of William himself; she disliked his manners, which were often casual and brusque, and what she described as his lack of principles and creed, by which apparently she meant his lack of orthodox beliefs. (This was something that later also slightly worried Queen Victoria.) Yet she had to admit that his conduct towards Caroline had been entirely honourable and that he had 'a thousand good qualities'. The day before the engagement was announced, and indeed before the matter had been finally settled, both mother and daughter seemed equally agitated. Caroline had received a letter from William which, when she showed it to her mother, almost won her over. Caroline, dramatic as ever, threw her arms round her mother's neck, declaring that she loved William better than anybody in the world but that she was prepared to give him up if her parents wished her so to do. This was an authority they were reluctant to use, fearing the effect such a refusal might have on their daughter's health, which had already been affected by the excess of emotion that the strain of loving him had produced. Matters were further complicated that emotion-packed morning when a letter came from the Duke of Devonshire saying that he hoped Caroline would marry his son Lord Hartington, her old nursery playmate and long her devoted slave. When later that evening the news was broken to the latter that she was definitely going to marry William the wretched young man threw a fit of hysterics, proclaiming that he had always thought of Caroline as his wife-to-be in the hope that once he had become of age his father would give his assent. Lord Hartington had in fact been afflicted with a bad attack of calf love.

The climax of this momentous day happened in the evening, when Lady Bessborough and Caroline attended a performance at Drury Lane. They had not seen William all day, a sense of propriety having prevented him from following up his letter in person, but Drury Lane was neutral ground and theatre boxes a recognised social rendezvous where William could approach his love. The warmth and animation of his manner were sufficient to vanquish any last doubts that Caroline might have entertained. According to her own account, much later given to Lady Morgan, though she had loved William for so long she was frightened of the violence of her own temper and had therefore hesitated to become his wife. (This statement may well have been due to hindsight as she looked backwards over their stormy marriage.) William had yet to discover whether Lady Bessborough would be as complaisant as her daughter and in order to speak to her privately he followed her out of the box. In response to his anxious question she told him that she and her husband had decided that this was a decision that Caroline herself must make. His feelings and relief overwhelmed him and throwing his arms round his future mother-in-law he kissed her. At that moment, most inopportunely, Canning accompanied by a friend appeared in the passage and William, overcome by confusion, turned and dashed down the stairs. Poor Lady Bessborough was almost equally embarrassed and to prevent ill-natured gossip she confided in Canning the reason for Lamb's impulsive action. Canning was all tact. He praised Lamb most generously and declared himself delighted at the news of the coming marriage, so that to some extent Lady Bessborough's doubts were removed. Nevertheless she was not completely happy about the marriage and would have liked the announcement of the engagement to have been deferred for a few days in order to give the young people the chance to reflect a little before finally committing themselves, for eighteenth-century engagements, once entered into, were difficult to break with decorum. But because they were so obviously devoted to each other and because his behaviour to her was everything that she could wish Lady Bessborough found her fears evaporating and she did grow to be warmly attached to him.

Long engagements were not the fashion and the wedding was fixed for 3 June. The days between were passed in a whirl of activities with streams of people coming to offer their congratulations and with endless hours spent with milliners and dressmakers. As the day drew near Caroline began to suffer from a characteristic depression. Her mother described her as low and frightened and on one occasion when the three of them were sitting together tried to rouse her from her dejection by saying that William would certainly think her unkind to show so much reluctance and so much fear at the prospect of leaving home. Caroline's rejoinder was that only people with unhappy homes could contemplate leaving them without regret and that the very fact that she was prepared to leave her beloved mother for him was in itself a sign of her great love. When it came to the actual ceremony, which took place at eight o'clock at night, Caroline was very nervous and upset as the time approached to leave Berkeley Square for her new home at Brocket. One can guess that if her later protestations of her ignorance before marriage were genuine, her passion for William was still the love of a romantic inexperienced girl who had suddenly realized that she had committed herself to she knew not what.

What passed between husband and wife can only be guessed. William can have been no inexperienced lover and throughout his life he showed to Caroline a tender and understanding love, but for a few days she was so shaken that she became ill, refusing to see anyone, even her mother. When Lady Bessborough paid her first visit to Brocket she found Caroline still in a nervous state but soon she was able to send a very cheerful report to Glanville Leveson Gower, saying how comfortable the newly married pair seemed together and how amazingly kind her new husband was to Caroline. It was a happy peaceful beginning to their life together. Generally the mornings were spent out and about but in the evenings William read aloud while mother and daughter sketched. With her lively mind Caroline made a receptive listener as her husband began to fill the gaps left by her haphazard education. (Later the pattern of these domestic evenings was to repeat itself with a more august young personage, Queen Victoria.) Lady Bessborough was reassured and delighted in her new son-in-law. However, she still remained uneasy about the rest of his family, observing wisely that one marries not only one's husband but all his relations; she felt that she could well dispense with some of these, though she dare not say so. The two mothers-in-law were old acquaintances. Lady Melbourne had contrived to make herself a welcome visitor at Devonshire House and it had been while Lady Bessborough and Caroline had been paying her a visit at Brocket that the latter had first met her future husband. Nevertheless the two women were widely different in temperament; both were intelligent, both deeply involved in contemporary politics, but Lady Bessborough was a softer, more vulnerable person, ruled in general by her heart rather than swayed by self interest. Lady Melbourne was discreet, cool, adept at cultivating the right people; a woman who never let her heart run away with her head. Lady Bessborough's nickname for her was 'the Thorn'. Outwardly Lady Melbourne had approved of the marriage, which spelt social advancement in that her favourite son had married the daughter of an earl, but she was certainly not the woman to appreciate Caroline's good qualities and had little sympathy with her moods, her extravagances and her utter disregard for convention. The future was to show her to be an unenthusiastic mother-in-law, though in so far as Caroline was more often a liability than a helpmate to William, as a mother she had some justification for the criticism and even disloyalty that marked her later attitude. It was not long after the marriage that an illuminating conversation took place between the two matrons. Lady Melbourne, adopting a semi-jocular manner, remarked to Lady Bessborough that she hoped that the daughter would turn out better than the mother (a sly allusion to her affair with Leveson Gower), or William might repent his choice. With commendable self-control Caroline's mother replied that with the help of Lady Melbourne's advice she hoped that she would, while nobly repressing a desire to allude to that lady's example, wherein as she well knew discretion was the better part of virtue.

In the early days and indeed years of their marriage, Lady Melbourne's fears seemed groundless. The young Lambs appeared blissfully happy, in spite of the sudden storms that sometimes blew up. Caroline's cousin Harriet Cavendish continually commented in her letters to her sister on the way in which marriage was improving her tempestuous cousin. She recorded that during a visit in July Caroline had become as gentle and poised as if she had been a country matron for twenty years instead of days. Even so Harriet found it difficult to think of her as a wife even though at the time she was fussing over William because he was not well; he had a cold and was suffering from toothache. Caroline herself was not strong and by December was experiencing her first pregnancy. Harriet, who never had a great deal of sympathy for her, reported that her cousin was terrified by a pain in her chest and was victimising all her friends by dwelling on her symptoms which everybody assured her were merely muscular pains. Possibly she had more grounds for her fears than Harriet was inclined to allow, as the child she was carrying was both premature and still-born. Nevertheless during her pregnancy Caroline seems to have been extraordinarily placid and content with such domestic pleasures as sharing a chair with her husband while reading out of the same book. Even so there were occasional quarrels, some of them violent, and often, as is not unusual in the early months of marriage, over trifles. On one occasion the matter in dispute was whether Caroline's maid Betsy should travel in the open or the closed carriage on their journey down to visit friends. William's temper was so ruffled that he left the house in annoyance, leaving a message that he should not be back until late that evening. Caroline's reaction was immediate. She sent her wedding ring home, covered herself with jewelry and rouged herself to the eyes before going to the play with Harriet, who sent an amusing account of the whole episode to her sister. There apparently she simmered down a little so that when her cousin deposited her at the Melbournes' house in Whitehall she seemed half indignant and half afraid. Caroline could never stand opposition and her manifestations of displeasure could be violent, ranging from bouts of near hysteria to snatching up the nearest piece of crockery and flinging it at her husband. In the early halcyon days of their marriage such sudden tantrums only produced ripples on the surface of what seemed and indeed was a very successful marriage.

Caroline was as yet utterly devoted to William and apparently most possessive in her loving. This appeared in all kinds of ways. When, for instance, the Lamb family, one of whose favourite pleasures was amateur theatricals, put on a play, in which William had to take the part of the lover, Harriet thought his somewhat tame performance was due to the fact that Caroline was watching him so closely that he feared to glance too tenderly at the woman with whom he was enacting a love scene for fear that his wife might throw a fit of hysteria. Even more embarrassing, according to the gossip of Caroline's maid, who passed it on to Harriet's woman, was her wifely habit, when her husband went to the 'piccola' or in straightforward English 'the little room', and stayed away longer than she thought he ought to have, of sending her maid to report whether he had in fact come straight back! As William's devotion was patent for everyone to see, and as he never seemed to leave her for an unnecessary moment, but seemed to love her more than ever, Harriet felt that her cousin might have spared herself the trouble. Whatever Caroline did she flung her whole being into it and the qualities of possessive passion that she displayed during the early years of her marriage were later to be repeated when she fell under the spell of Lord Byron.

During these first years, apart from sudden flare-ups, which Caroline could never control and which burnt out as quickly as they burst into flame, the only shadow to fall on the young couple was the birth of their still-born child on 6 January, a premature baby of seven months. By the end of the year she was pregnant again and her son was born on 11 September 1807. There were great rejoicings; the child was christened Augustus and the Prince Regent graced the christening. At first all appeared to be well. Augustus was an exceptionally large and healthy child and Caroline threw herself with her usual wild enthusiasm into the role of a mother. Harriet reported that the company heard of nothing but the beauty and strength and size of the infant and of Caro's rapture. In spite of the inevitable train of nurses and under-nurses she nursed the child herself and, with her nervous apprehensions and moods behind her for a time, blossomed into happy motherhood. Yet even here she had to overplay her part. Taking the child out became not a simple airing but a ceremony. She would ride with the child on her lap, a page in full uniform holding the horse's bridle, with nurses and nursemaids following on foot behind, all to the mirth of the turnpike men as she passed. In other ways too she was beginning to develop eccentricities, frequenting a box at the theatre accompanied only by a favourite page, and making herself conspicuous by her disregard of accepted conventions.

Her nervous instability demanded constant change and variety; there must always be some fresh outlet for her emotional urges, some new role for her to play. When the Lambs were staying with the Gloucesters at Cowes, Harriet (who, it is apparent from reading between the lines of her letters, seems to have rather disliked both of them previously but whose sympathies were now turning towards William) commented on their restless life, visiting, riding, boating. She described them as leading the life of characters in a Harlequinade with patient William for ever waving his wand in order to fulfil Columbine's slightest wish, so that Lady Spencer, Caroline's grandmother, dubbed him an angel. Nevertheless by 1809 even his wings seemed to be growing a little weary.

It is not that he had ceased to love Caroline or she him in her fashion, but life was no longer running quite as smoothly or as pleasantly as when he first became a husband and an MP. Politics were proving increasingly unrewarding when William was not only in opposition but in an opposition with which he was only half in agreement. His son too did not make the progress, except in a purely physical way, that a child of two might have been expected to show; his eyes were tiny and he had an odd helpless look. Then in February 1809 Caroline had another miscarriage which to some extent may explain her increased restlessness. Moreover the situation was not helped by the fact that she fitted badly into the Lamb family who, though they had eccentricities enough of their own, had little patience with the forms that hers took, while to Caroline admiration and approbation were as necessary as the air she breathed. Too loyal to criticise his wife, William began to ponder on marriage as an institution, writing in his commonplace book that the main reason against it was that 'two minds, however congenial they may be and however submissive one may be to the other, can never act like one' adding ruefully: 'Before I was married, whenever I saw the children or the dogs allowed, or rather encouraged to be troublesome in a house, I used to lay it all to the fault of the master of it, who might at once put a stop to it if he pleased. Since I married I find that this was a very rash and premature judgment.' William once told Queen Victoria that he thought no man ought to marry before he was thirty and that he himself was quite unready to deal with its strains when he married. In these years he had come face to face with reality and with far more justification could now have composed some lines from an earlier poem:

> We find that those who every transport know,
> In full proportion taste of every woe . . .

Worse was to come, making the following lines prophetic:

> The work of wretchedness is never done,
> And misery's sigh extends with every sun.

Until the close of 1809, though Caroline had been an exasperating and worrying wife, showing, as Byron was to tell her later, 'a total want of common conduct', her husband was still 'dearest William' and no other man had supplanted him in her affections. After quarrels and displays of temperament she would promise to amend her ways, declaring that she would 'be silent of a morning, entertaining after dinner; docile' and taking the blame for their differences on herself. Then for a few days they would resume their old happy relations. If William was not experiencing the total happiness that he had envisaged when Caroline had accepted him, he had learnt to live with her moods, moderating them when he could, comforting her when the storm of hysteria or despair had passed and showing her a depth of understanding that could only have been born of a deep and genuine love. But Caroline needed something more exciting than this. In some ways the relationship between the Lambs resembled that between Victoria and her 'angel' Albert. She too, like Caroline, was given to self-will and violent rages though, unlike her, she neither threw crockery nor rolled in paroxysms of fury and misery on the ground, but she might have found her nervous outbursts less shattering if Albert had been less infuriatingly patient. It could be argued that a sharp slap judiciously administered would have done neither woman any harm. In Regency England no court of law, and probably few people, would have questioned a husband's right to deal with a troublesome wife in this way but this was a remedy that a man of William's temperament could never employ. He was too gentle and too kind. To someone like Caroline the situation lacked romance and excitement. She was never a woman to thank heaven fasting for a good man's love. As a steady diet she found William dull. She began to crave for forbidden fruit, if only for the excitement of stealing it. She had always been able to attract men. The Duke of Devonshire confessed to finding her very entertaining while admitting that in general she appealed more to men than to women. In 1810 her craving for excitement began to make her look elsewhere. She enjoyed the emotion of being in love. She does not seem to have been a sensual woman driven on by physical urges so much as one whose satisfaction came more from being ecstatically happy and absorbed in another being, or of being in the depths of misery, than from the fulfilment of that love. This, presumably, she had found with William in the first happy years of their marriage; after five years it was not enough to satisfy her ego.

The men on whom she now chose to concentrate her affections were as different as possible from her husband, though after each misadventure it was always to the security of his love that she returned. Her first serious entanglement was in 1810 when she fancied herself in love with Sir Godfrey Webster, Lady Holland's son by her first marriage, who, as the antithesis of William, may therefore have satisfied some deep-seated need within her. He too was handsome but cast in a coarser mould, intellectually quite unsubtle, and unlikely for that reason to satisfy Caroline's more finely attuned mind for long. He was a confessed loose-liver; a man who boasted of his success with women and had little beyond this self-proclaimed vitality to recommend him to the discerning. Caroline flung herself in his path with her usual whole-hearted commitment; they were seen together everywhere. Her infatuation could not but have appealed to his vanity and in addition, though this is pure conjecture, Sir Godfrey may not have been unwilling to create a scandal around the wife of a man of whom his mother was so fond. From 1799 Lamb had been a welcome visitor at Holland House, and much later young Queen Victoria was to show some jealousy when he spent time there which she considered should have been lavished on her.

Tongues soon began to wag over Caroline's affair and the three mothers involved, Lady Holland, Lady Bessborough and Lady Melbourne, all in their different ways tried to drill a little discretion and prudence into her. Lady Melbourne bitterly upbraided her daughter-in-law for her failure to be discreet since her behaviour, with its undertones of scandal, could not but harm William's position in the Commons. In self defence or retaliation – no-one can ever be reasonably sure of her chameleon motives since she lied not only to the world but to herself – Caroline tried to throw the blame on William, protesting that she had brought an almost childlike innocence and inexperience to marriage, and that it was he who had called her prudish and made fun of her straight-laced outlook. How much credence can be given to this assertion it is difficult to know. In Regency England the gulf between the unmarried girl and the married woman was a deep one. Young girls of good family, like their counterparts in early twentieth-century Spain and France, led cloistered lives; to lose their virginity before marriage meant the destruction of every hope of a respectable match and a fitting establishment, but it is still difficult to believe that when Caroline accompanied her mother to Paris in the brief interval of peace secured by the Peace of Amiens this innocence, based on ignorance, could have remained intact. Undoubtedly Lady Bessborough did her best to shelter her daughter from the gossip that connected her own name with that of Leveson Gower, and Caroline's own romantic ideals may have provided an impenetrable shelter against malicious innuendo, but if she remained unaware of the amorous adventures that were taking place around her, such innocence could not long have survived marriage even if her husband had done nothing to enlighten her. A married woman, visiting fashionable houses, taking her full share of the social whirl of London, could hardly have been oblivious of the gossip, the *'on dit'* of the day, and her husband's attempts to open her eyes to the realities behind the gracious facade may well have been made in order to cushion her against the shock of discovery rather than to destroy her illusions, though William may have underestimated the shock that this would be to her. The atmosphere of the Lamb household was robustly materialistic and his sister Emily, now the wife of Lord Cowper, was far more fitted to take an unblinkered view of life than poor romantic Caro, who later was to describe herself as a stranded 'gay, merry little boat, or a butterfly scorched but not killed in the flame of a tallow candle.' The latter simile is the more accurate, but underlying both is the feeling of helplessness. It was her realisation of this that after every crisis made her return to William, her one sure anchor, her one rescuer from the flame of her own egotism.

Perhaps it was his long experience of Caroline that endowed

him with the capacity to do nothing even when circumstances seemed to demand action and when his colleagues pressed him to take it. Every problem left to itself, he would argue, solved itself; letters left unanswered long enough ceased to require an answer. By 1810 he had learned the futility of trying to control his wife; his role was to institute salvage operations. All that he could hope to do was to damp down gossip by seeming oblivious of a situation about which he could do nothing. Throughout the crises of Caroline's emotional life he went to the House as usual and affected to notice nothing. Perhaps he, better than anyone, knew how much smoke and how little flame of passion there were in the fires that his wife was so busily fanning. Nevertheless, though he ignored it, he must have hated the gossip. How deeply the possibility of her unfaithfulness disturbed him there is no means of knowing. So long as the decencies were preserved adultery was scarcely frowned upon in contemporary society. Emily's name was constantly linked with that of the young Tory Secretary of War, Lord Palmerston; neither his own mother nor Caroline's were faithful to their marriage vows. Even if Caroline were physically unfaithful, morally she was no worse than many of the Devonshire House circle. Her fault was to defy convention; something she had always gloried in doing. This was not a quality that would commend itself to anyone like Lady Melbourne, or even to her son, though his own abrupt manners and lavish use of 'damn' did not put him beyond criticism. Nevertheless it was open to two interpretations, one sympathetic to Lady Caroline, one condemnatory. To her detractors everything that she did was done for effect. She outraged conventions because she wanted to be the centre of every picture. Kinder critics have credited her with scorning convention as a sham and the enemy of genuine emotion. She believed, they argue, in the duty of self-expression and might have taken as her motto that if true to oneself 'thou canst not then be false to any man'. This is perhaps too favourable a gloss. It was the picture that she wished to present to the world, at the most a half truth. The key to her behaviour was her egotism.

Caroline's infatuation with Sir Godfrey was of short duration. With what philosophy William comforted himself in the meantime can only be surmised. Would the prevalence of adultery within his own family condition him to accept it in his wife or did he judge her public infatuation to be merely another manifestation of her restless, sensation-loving nature? It is difficult to believe that he was as unmoved as outwardly he appeared. Any man who had loved as deeply as William Lamb had loved his young wife must have grieved at finding himself no longer the most important man in her life, whether physically she had been unfaithful or not. However, if he relied on the volatile nature of Caroline's affections he was soon justified by events. It is possible that she was already beginning to be bored with her latest conquest when chance presented her with the opportunity to make a dramatic break with Sir Godfrey. One day when playing with Augustus a dog which her admirer had given to her snapped at the child. With horror she saw that the animal was foaming at the mouth. Convulsed with terror lest the dog were mad, and convinced that if the boy had died it would have been God's judgment on his erring mother, Caroline gave herself up to an orgy of remorse and the baronet faded out of her life, to the great relief of her family and her husband. Unfortunately worse was to follow.

'Childe Harold' had been published in the February of 1812 and overnight Byron had become the idol of London society. With his auburn hair, blue grey eyes and dramatically pale handsome face he became the most sought after man in London. It was inevitable that he and Caroline should meet, and all but inevitable that, suffering as she was from an emotional vacuum, she should fall under his spell. 'Childe Harold' was full of dark hints of wickedness, with lines such as 'For he through Sin's long labyrinth had run', and 'He felt the fulness of satiety', and everything Caroline heard about Lord Byron heightened the effect that his poetry had produced. Yet in their first celebrated meeting at Lady Jersey's ball she turned away without a word, later making her much-quoted judgment that he was 'mad, bad and dangerous to know.' If this was a premonition of the misery he was to cause her it was one which she soon disregarded. Two days later they met again at Holland House; Byron asked permission to call, this was given, he then asked to see her alone, this request too she granted and by the end of the week Caroline had abandoned herself to the full flood of her feelings. She and Byron went everywhere together; after parties she drove back in his carriage; they exchanged flowers, his gift a rose and a carnation, hers a sunflower symbolising that he was now her sun. Once again tongues wagged as Caroline flaunted her infatuation to the world.

The extent to which Byron returned her passion is more difficult to evaluate. After a thwarted childhood and early manhood when, as an impoverished peer, he had been largely ignored by the society in which he felt he had the right to move, his first poems, 'Hours of Idleness', had been savagely criticised when he published them in 1807. Before the publication of 'Childe Harold' he had become a young man with an outsized chip on his shoulder, humiliated by a lack of recognition and sensitively self-conscious of his club foot. Then in his own words 'I awoke one morning and found myself famous.' To have lived in a cellar and then to be flung into the full glare of the noonday midsummer sun means that everything has to be refocussed with eyes still dazzled by the new radiance. So it must have been with Byron. Hitherto his vanity had been starved; now he was greedy for everything that could feed it. Adoration from Lady Caroline was satisfying in two ways. Because she was the daughter of an earl she gratified his desire for social recognition, and as a newcomer on the social scene he was probably unaware of the gossip her affair with Sir Godfrey had already caused. Moreover, though women of her physical type did not generally attract him, Caroline could be a fascinating companion; with her quick apprehension and darting mind she was almost a burning flame on the altar of his own egotism. But however much his vanity was flattered he soon began to tire of an adoration so possessive and so demanding. Both Byron and Caroline were supreme egotists. She too wrote verses and was hungry for Byron to praise them, while he wanted only her praise for his own. They had in reality very little to give one another. Moreover Lady Melbourne began to play a skilful hand in the game.

There was very little that she did not know about men. She liked them, she understood their point of view and now she laid herself out to attract Byron and to win his confidence. She was always a superb listener and her tactics were successful. The next step was easy. After one of Caroline's scenes Lady Melbourne was always at hand, ready to laugh, to sympathise and to work gently on the bonds that still tied him to her daughter-in-law. Byron grew cooler, though whether Caroline herself had worn him out or whether Lady Melbourne's skill had borne fruit is difficult to decide. As he became cooler Caroline grew more frantic at the prospect of losing him. To apportion blame for the conduct of both the lovers, if indeed lovers they were, is impossible. Judging by his early letters and words Byron too had been, at least temporarily, very much in love, but the words of a poet cannot necessarily be accepted as genuine evidence of his feelings. Declarations of passion and of undying fidelity were what Caroline demanded, and under emotional pressure they were not difficult to give, however embarrassing the gift might afterwards prove to be to the giver. Had Caroline not been married, perhaps in a sudden surge of feeling Byron might have agreed to marriage, but married or not there could never have been a happy ending to their story. Only a great love and deep understanding, such as William had shown towards her, could have coped with Caroline's emotions. Byron could no more have adjusted his egotism to Caroline's than she was able to do to his.

4
ENDS AND
BEGINNINGS

IT might have been better if at this time Byron had nerved himself to make a complete break, instead of which he tried, in a way that at times seems curiously half-hearted, to escape more gradually from a situation that was becoming increasingly embarrassing. His motives can only be surmised; probably they were as mixed as those of any man caught in a similar trap. Their early attraction had been mutual and he and Caroline had been very close to one another. Whether they had actually been lovers has never been definitely established; even their own testimony must remain suspect, for both of them twisted their memories to the emotion of the moment. Meanwhile Caroline, her nerves raw with uncertainty, grew more hysterical, giving way to the violence of her distress in prolonged bouts of sobbing, interspersed with such incidents as her sudden impulse to escape from her misery by heedless, headlong flight. Lady Bessborough was almost ill with worry about her daughter's state, which seemed to defy all maternal attempts to restrain or comfort her. Things reached a climax when on 13 August she called at Melbourne House (all this time Caroline continued to reside with her husband under the family roof) only to be confronted by a frantic Lord Melbourne looking, she said, as pale as death and screaming to the porter to stop Caroline who had just dashed out of the house in a moment of furious temper. Apparently in one of her hysterical outbursts she had threatened to seek refuge with Byron and her exasperated father-in-law had told her to go and be damned, adding the wounding comment that he did not think Byron would take her. For Caroline this was the final insult; she ran headlong down the street. At first all three, Lady Bessborough and Lord and Lady Melbourne – there is no mention of William being present – thought that once she had cooled down she would return. When she did not, in desperation the two ladies drove to Byron's, fearing that she had carried out her threat and thrown herself on his protection. To their great relief she was not there; indeed he seemed as frightened as they were at her impulsive action, which he had every right to be. The last thing he wanted was to be involved in a public scandal.

While the two mothers were searching for her, Caroline had first dashed into a neighbouring chemist's to avoid being seen. She then sold a ring and with the money hired a hackney cab to drive her to Kensington, where she borrowed another £20 on a second ring. With this money she meant to travel on the stage road, in itself a most unconventional thing for a woman in her position to have done, to Portsmouth where she intended to take a passage on the first boat that she could find regardless of its destination. Unfortunately for her plan she paid the hackney coachman to leave a packet of letters with Byron's servant and on receiving these Byron acted immediately. He traced the coachman, who by a mixture of bribes and threats was persuaded to drive the poet back to the house where he had left Caroline, which belonged to a surgeon, from whose care Byron, under the pretence that he was her brother, almost forcibly removed her back to Cavendish Square. Between them they persuaded her to return to her husband's house. Lady Bessborough went in first, fearful that the Lambs would no longer receive her daughter, and now found William there. Of his feelings and his actions during these hectic hours there is no record, but to Lady Bessborough's enormous relief William showed himself once again ready to forgive. By now he must have realised that his wife was no longer completely responsible for her actions and have accepted the burden that her obsessional behaviour imposed on him. In the next months he did everything possible to keep his 'gay, merry, little boat' from destroying herself utterly against the rocks of her despair.

The immediate problem was to get her away. Previous to her

latest exploit her mother had been trying to persuade her to go back with her to Roehampton, where she would have had no easy opportunity to seek out Byron, and from there, accompanied by William, to visit first the Bessborough estates in Ireland and then Lismore castle, the Cavendishes' place. Indeed it may have been this plan that had persuaded Caroline, who dreaded the contrived separation, that her only resource was to throw herself on Byron's protection. The immediate consequence of her escapade had been to upset her mother to the point of collapse, so that her housekeeper, an old and valued retainer, so far forgot her station as to write to Caroline reproaching her for the unhappiness she had caused to her mistress. Predictably Caroline swung from defiance to a morass of self-reproach, in which she promised to go to Ireland as originally planned. Even then she still equivocated and delayed, arguing that though she would indeed go to Roehampton the journey to Ireland must be delayed until her mother was fit to undertake it. She even implied that she was again pregnant. Whether this was deception or wishful thinking there is no means of ascertaining; there had been two miscarriages since the birth of Augustus and she knew how much her husband longed for another child. So it was not until early September that the family set out. Byron's conduct at this time was very ambiguous; some people would call it caddish. But otherwise how was he ever to be free of Caroline? Earlier in the year he had discussed with Lady Melbourne the idea of marrying, partly as a method of breaking free and partly out of a desire for a secure emotional anchorage, and she had suggested a young kinswoman of her own, Arabella Milbanke, as a suioable bride. It was in some ways a curious choice for so experienced a woman to make. Admittedly Miss Milbanke was an heiress and Byron was short of money, moreover he wanted an anchor and she was a young woman of principle. But she was not the type either to turn Byron into a faithful husband or to bear with him if he strayed, and one would have expected Lady Melbourne to realise this. Possibly her own motives were not unmixed; she wanted to avert scandal from her son, and she was possibly not anxious to hand Byron to a wife over whom she could not hope to have control and who would leave no place in his life for his erstwhile confidante.

Byron duly proposed and was rejected, but so kindly that he

and Arabella continued to meet on friendly terms. Marriage not being immediately available as a refuge he turned to the slightly tarnished Lady Oxford for amorous consolation, going down to stay with her at Eyewood in October. Nevertheless for a time he continued to write to Caroline, now in Ireland, letters that breathed a constant devotion intended to soothe and calm her, while at the same time trying to persuade her that for the sake of her family they must part. But he realised that the deception could not go on and he informed Lady Melbourne, probably in September, that he did not intend to write again. Having refrained from so doing for three weeks he received one of Caroline's tempestuous letters, half offering to give him up. This he found so difficult to answer that having thrown his attempt into the fire he continued to take refuge in silence. This had the predictable effect of both terrifying and infuriating Caroline, who showered him with letters until in a final effort to shake her off he sent an irritated and cruelly worded letter starting 'I am no longer your lover' and ending 'I offer you this advice, correct your vanity, which is ridiculous; exert your absurd caprices upon others, and leave me in peace', while declaring that he would remain her friend. This was the letter in which, by incorporating it in her novel *Glenarvon*, she published her humiliation to the world. Undaunted, Caroline continued to press for a meeting, perhaps with the hope that face to face she could win back his love, perhaps only to relieve her own pent-up misery. Meanwhile she demanded that he should send back the presents that she had sent him in exchange for those which he had given her. When he refused, confessing to Lady Melbourne that by now he did not in fact know what had become of half of them, the distraught Caroline held a public bonfire at Brocket, burning ceremonially both his presents and his letters, much as the public hangman might burn blasphemous or seditious literature.

Yet even this was not the end. There was to be one more public display of her frustrated passion. Caroline continued to go into society; so did Byron. On 5 July 1813 they both attended Lady Heathcote's ball. When the band struck up for the waltz Lady Caroline was asked to lead it. Byron's views on waltzing were well known. In Regency England this dance was an innovation of which many people, brought up on the old country dances and the stately minuets and gavottes, disapproved on moral grounds. Queen Victoria as a young woman always sat out the waltz until she danced it with Prince Albert, and Lord Melbourne, as he then was, approved of her restraint. Was he, one wonders, remembering what took place at Lady Heathcote's ball? Before the advent of Byron Caroline had been a most enthusiastic addict of the waltz but Byron, either from physical fastidiousness or, more probably, from pique because his deformed foot prevented him from mastering its steps, had condemned it publicly in his poem 'The Waltz', castigating the way in which

> Round all the confines of the yielded waist,
> The stranger's hand may wander undisplaced

and prophesying that

> The breast thus publicly resigned to man,
> In private may resist him – if it can.

Once Lady Caroline had fallen under his spell she had ceased to waltz and it was half as an act of defiance, half possibly with the hope that to see her in another man's arms might reawaken his jealousy, that, seeing Byron standing by, she accosted him with the question, 'I suppose I may take the floor now?' His answer, as she might have foreseen, was an expression of indifference, a public snub that was in itself enough to cause gossip. Worse was to follow. What happened later in the supper room is not clear; subsequently there were too many accounts which do not agree as to the details. According to one account Byron, seeing her handle a knife in a suspicious manner, told her to turn it on herself not him, and in fury she slashed her wrist until the blood came; in another story she broke a glass and was deliberately cutting her arm with it; in a third, her own, a glass was accidentally broken and her arm scratched with it. Byron, writing to Lady Melbourne next day, said he had not been in the supper room at the time the incident took place and that he had only heard about it later. The gossip was that Caroline had tried to commit suicide, which she, in a later letter to Lady Morgan, denied. Whatever the truth all London buzzed with this new scandal. The humiliation of the Lamb family can well be imagined.

In spite of the unenviable notoriety that was beginning to cling to his wife's name William continued to protect her as best he could against both the world and herself. In the summer of 1814 the pair were in Paris celebrating with the rest of fashionable society the return of the Bourbon king Louis XVIII. Caroline seems to have recovered some of her enjoyment of life but the Kembles, through an uncurtained window, saw at least one of her bouts of fury when, unsuccessful in getting her own way, she flung the china at her husband's head. Back in London later that summer it was impossible to prevent Caroline from trying to force herself on Byron once again. On a visit to his chambers in the Albany, where she found him absent but with the novel *Vathek* by William Beckford lying on the table, impulsively she wrote on the fly leaf the words 'Remember me', an act that called forth the well-known bitter poem:

> Remember thee, remember thee!
> Till Lethe quench life's burning stream
> Remorse and shame shall cling to thee
> And haunt thee like a feverish dream.
>
> Remember thee! Ay, doubt it not,
> Thy husband too shall think of thee,
> By neither shalt thou be forgot,
> Thou false to him, thou fiend to me!

Wild and unrestrained though Lady Caroline's behaviour had been, one cannot help but feel that some of the 'remorse and shame' might cling to Byron, though she had made him pay dearly for the brief months of her fascination for him and though the most brutal behaviour on his part was ineffective in shaking her off. Yet when he finally escaped from her by marrying Arabella Milbanke, Caroline showed herself capable of generous feelings. After some anxious deliberation she sent a wedding present, and when, barely a year after the marriage, London society buzzed again, this time with the rumour that Lord and Lady Byron were to separate, she wrote to him several times urging a reconciliation and arguing that a separation could only damage his reputation, as by now she realised that her own public display of passion had damaged hers. This generous impulse bore no fruit; Byron left England and his wife for ever, but in 1821, by a last ironic twist of fate, while out driving she encountered the funeral procession bringing back his body from Greece.

During the intervening years Caroline, like a wounded bird, had fluttered from one distressing episode to another. William's attitude to his wife's vagaries remained inscrutable. He ate his usual hearty meals, his laugh was as boisterous as ever, his manner in public remained unchanged. Caroline in a self-excusing autobiographical sketch which she sent to Lady Morgan declared: 'He cared nothing for my morals. I might flirt and go about with whatsoever man I pleased. He was privy to my affair with Lord Byron, and laughed at it. His indolence rendered him insensible to everything. When I ride, play and amuse him he loves me. In sickness and suffering he deserts me. His violence is as bad as my own.' Such assertions were both unjust and untrue, as in her more balanced moments she well knew. She was nearer to the truth when she wrote, also to Lady Morgan, that after her wild attempt to run away 'William at that time, loved me so much that he forgave me all and only implored me to remain.' Yet this was at the height of the Byron affair. Because William insisted on standing by Caroline his sister Emily and the rest of the family did their best to save her from social ostracism. But as Caroline's behaviour became more and more unbalanced the slow pressure of family disapproval began to wear away his reluctance to agree to a legal separation. Not one of his near relations approved of Caroline. Even Lord Egremont declared that 'the only blunder he could never understand was his mad choice of a wife' adding, 'I always thought he had better judgement and taste.'

By 1816 there was an additional reason why he should free himself from the embarrassment inseparable from a life with Caroline. He was offered a safe seat at Northampton and his family and friends alike were anxious that he should resume his parliamentary career. Yet even after he had decided to take their advice there was a certain half-heartedness both in terminating his conjugal life and in resuming his political one. Four years of watching the disintegration of his wife and of the political party to which he belonged had encouraged the cynicism that was to mark his later years; perhaps disillusion might be a more accurate word. Increasingly he had found both relaxation and stimulation in his library at Brocket, where he could close the door on all the perplexities that crowded in on him and retreat into the intricacies of theology as debated by the Fathers, or refresh himself with the delights of Greek and Latin Authors.

His old friend Lord Holland, as well as his mother, had been anxious for him to return to the House of Commons ever since he had declined to offer himself for re-election in 1812. This William had been reluctant to do, at least partly because his political loyalties were no longer whole-heartedly with his Whig friends, or indeed with any one group of politicians. After 1815 Lamb found himself more and more in sympathy with men like George Canning, who, having left his own Whig principles far behind, had become what could be described as a moderate Tory. Though Lamb approved of the principle of Roman Catholic Emancipation, as did Canning, he was sceptical of the vague ideas on reform which the Whigs, in theory, were supposed to favour. All that he wanted, perhaps all that he ever wanted in politics, was a strong Britain abroad and a stable society at home. When therefore he re-entered the House as MP for Northampton in 1816 it was as a man bound by social ties to his old friends, who were mainly Whigs – even though these were split into groups, the Grenvillites and Lord Grey's supporters by no means seeing eye to eye – but politically by no means hostile to Lord Liverpool's administration, particularly after Canning joined it as President of the Board of Control in June 1816.

For a time it looked as if the renewal of his political life might also see the end of his married life. Arrangements for a judicial separation were put in train. Caroline was in despair and in this mood of desperation, as some relief to her overcharged emotions, in three weeks she produced the novel with which her name is usually associated, *Glenarvon*. Set in the dramatic framework of the contemporary Gothic novel and written at white-hot speed, it was full of every kind of improbability. Wild though the story was, the theme was predictably autobiographical. Her description of the hero, Glenarvon, was her conception of Byron writ large: 'The eye beamed into life as it threw its dark, ardent gaze with a look nearly of inspiration, while the proud curl of the upper lip expressed harshness and bitter contempt; yet, even mixed with these fierce characteristic feelings, an air of melancholy and dejection shaded and softened every harsher expression. Such a countenance spoke to the heart and filled it with one vague yet powerful interest, so strong, so indefinable that it could not be easily overcome.' It is perhaps not surprising that even Byron found it wearing to live up to this portrayal for more than a few months. Had Caroline confined herself to emotion-packed descriptions of the suffering of the heroine, so clearly intended to be herself, and of the villain-hero, equally clearly intended to be Byron, the novel, though it could not have failed to become a talking point in fashionable society when it was published in the May of 1816, might have created less resentment against its authoress if it had not also contained some devastating caricatures of various prominent London hostesses, including William's close friend Lady Holland.

Though it was published anonymously the authorship of *Glenarvon* was no secret. The Melbournes were both furious and humiliated and William in deep distress of spirit told his wife: 'I have stood your friend till now – I even think you ill used; but if it is true this novel is published – and, as they say, against us all – I will never see you more.' It was a resolution which he found himself unable to keep. Caroline's own defence was her misery; to write the novel, she declared, had been her sole comfort, and when she had allowed its publication it was because she thought herself 'ruined beyond recall.' William knew her well enough to accept her attempts at exculpation and when the social pack bayed for her destruction his never completely dormant instinct to protect her was once more aroused. As Caroline herself wrote to Lord Glanville: 'He saw and feels deeply the unpleasant situation it is for him, but he loves me enough to stand firm as a rock.' If love it still was it was a very different love from the ecstatic rapture that had made him fling his arms round his future mother-in-law behind the box in Drury Lane. By 1816 he seems – and one must be content with such words, to have felt the futility of most things. Was it worth all the unpleasantness of a judicial separation when freedom promised nothing positive in the way of happiness and when it must destroy the woman he had once so ardently loved? Even so, urged on by his family he might have gone through with it had not Caroline followed him back to Brocket and, by what cajolery cannot be known, won him back to the extent of his refusing to sign the deed of separation when the lawyers brought it to him next morning.

Outwardly the Lambs picked up their life again and Caroline was seen at the opera, or waltzing at balls. She dabbled in politics, throwing herself into the business of getting William's youngest brother George returned for Westminster, one of the few popular constituencies, when he stood for election in 1819. The year before had brought fresh grief to William with the death of his mother. The link between them had always been strong, though he had not always taken her advice; now he was more alone than ever except for the affection of his sister Emily. In 1821 Caroline suffered a similar loss with the death of Lady Bessborough. By that year there seemed little light in the sky. Though William insisted on engaging a tutor for his son, Augustus was quite incapable mentally of mastering the Classics which his father so doggedly continued to hope that he could. During these years his relenting over Caroline brought little happiness to him or stability to her. Old friends treated her with coldness, so that she was driven to seek others in the literary world, women like Lady Morgan the Irish novelist, and William Godwin the philosopher. Her own subsequent·novels, 'Graham Hamilton', published in 1820 and 'Ada Reis' in 1823 were only moderately successful. She could still attract men but now they were the young and inexperienced ones, youths like Bulwer Lytton, who while still a student at Cambridge had a fit of calf love for her, until he was ousted from his position as favourite by an illegitimate son of the Duke of Bedford. When life grew too boring or too frustrating Caroline now took refuge in the brandy bottle rather than in golden dreams. By 1825 William accepted the hopelessness of the situation, worn down by his wife's unpredictable behaviour and constant violent scenes. He could take no more and this time the deed of separation was signed. Once again Caroline seemed shattered, pouring out her despair to Lady Morgan. 'Pity me' she wrote, 'for I am too unhappy. I cannot bear it. I would give all that I possessed on earth to be again what I once was, and I would now be obedient and gentle; but I shall die of grief.' Exile from Brocket was a terrible prospect, though she was still sufficiently resilient to fight for an adequate maintenance while writing of herself as one driven out of her beloved home to live in squalid poverty. This at least was an imaginary danger; William made adequate financial arrangements and for a short time, to the immeasurable relief of his family, Caroline went to Paris. But even to the last William could never completely harden his heart towards her. In a few months she went back at Brocket with her son for company, though while she lived William no longer made it his home.

The last two years of her life after her return to Brocket provided an oddly tranquil sunset to their stormy marriage. Though she was only forty her slight frame had been worn out by the violence that blazed within her. William rode over to see her often and they wrote one another quiet, gentle, affectionate letters. At the end, as at the beginning, he was her 'dear William'. To Lady Morgan she listed the priorities of her love as 'William Lamb first, my mother second, Byron third, my boy fourth.' When she became ill with what proved to be dropsy William was in Ireland, and her one desire was to live long enough to see him again. 'In this,' in her brother's words, 'she was gratified and was still able to converse with him and enjoy his society, but for the past three days it was apparent that her strength was declining, and on Sunday night, about nine o'clock she expired without a struggle.' Throughout her illness, which, when its serious nature had been realized, had caused her to be moved back to Melbourne House, the scene of so many of their dramas, Lady Caroline had shown a fortitude and a courage that had surprised all those who were around her. With her death one chapter in William Lamb's life was irrevocably closed. The effect and strain of these years can only be guessed. Now he was free. A new start was possible. Had he still the enthusiasm to make one, or would he merely drift, letting events dictate his path, at once too unambitious and too indolent to carve one out for himself through the wilderness of possibilities that surrounded him?

Though William Lamb had resumed his interrupted political career in 1816 he had pursued it with a noticeable lack of enthusiasm and diligence, attending the House spasmodically and speaking rarely. As usual he was torn both ways, loyalty to his Whig friends – it would be scarcely accurate to describe them as a party, so divided were they among themselves on matters of policy – kept him in opposition though frequently he found himself more in sympathy with the government. On the assassination of Spencer Perceval in 1812 Lord Liverpool had assumed the thankless role of Prime Minister. His administration was not expected to last but when Liverpool had a stroke in 1827 he was still Prime Minister. The Whigs had been in the political wilderness for twenty years. They had been difficult years both for the government and for the people of Britain. When he succeeded Perceval the French wars had hardly turned in her favour, then came the problem of making a satisfactory peace and as far as possible of harvesting the fruits of victory, which, as so often happens, proved to be bitter fruits for many people as the economy had to be readjusted from the needs of war to those of peace. In 1815 this problem was made more difficult of solution because by the early decades of the nineteenth century Britain was experiencing the so-called 'industrial revolution' which was accompanied by a social revolution as traditional ways of thinking about the structure of society were challenged. The cotton industry moved into the factories, followed rather more slowly by the woollen. Iron was being mass produced in furnaces and forges fired by coal. The steam engine was making things possible that had never been possible before. The agricultural interest, for so long the base of both the economic and the social life of the country, was losing ground to a capitalist mass-produced industry. Villages were becoming manufacturing towns; old commercial centres, such as Manchester and Liverpool, were growing into vast, insanitary, urban sprawls. The population was growing at an alarming rate so that the land could no longer supply all the food that was needed if the harvest happened to be a poor one. The result of change, though it spelled opportunity for some, brought hardship and misery to the majority of working people. After a brief post-war boom unemployment was heavy as wartime demand fell away and overseas markets, in the throes of their own post-war reconstruction, were too poor to absorb the massive new productivity of the new industry. In towns like Birmingham, geared to wartime production, in 1818 it was stated in Parliament that one fifth of the inhabitants were on poor relief.

The result was widespread disorder. Throughout the early years of the Liverpool administration ministers felt that they were sitting on a powder keg which migh blow society as they knew it to pieces. In 1812 there was much machine breaking as unemployed workpeople blamed their plight on the new labour-saving machinery and struggled to destroy it under the mythical leadership of one Ludd. During the depression of 1816 a large working-class rally at Spa Fields degenerated into a mob that became a riot, while the starving weavers of Manchester tried to march to London to present their case. Magistrates in the industrial areas bombarded the Home Office with rumours of men drilling on the moors of the North. Agitators were blamed for the riots and petitions which in most cases had no other cause than unemployment and semi-starvation. Everywhere the old order was being challenged, new classes were demanding a share of political power. In 1819 a gigantic rally organised to promote these aims was held on Peterloo Fields in Manchester, an occasion which, due more to panic and mismanagement on the part of the magistrates than to any evil design, led to the yeomanry charging the crowd so that lives were lost and the antagonism between the masses and their rulers developed a new bitterness. In 1820 an extremist, Arthur Thistlewood, planned to assassinate the Cabinet. The Government tried to make some adjustments in the Corn Laws but by returning to the Gold Standard after wartime non-convertibility it possibly made the post-war depression worse, though this is arguable. Governments main preoccupation continued to be with the maintenance of Law and Order. After the Spa Fields riots Habeas Corpus was suspended, Lamb voting with the Government, but when, after the fury aroused among radicals and the masses by Peterloo, the Government introduced a new series of acts which severely limited the right to demonstrate and protest, he supported Lord Althrop's Whig motion calling for a special committee to inquire into the state of the country on the grounds that further restrictive measures might only produce another Peterloo.

After 1822 the situation eased as the economic outlook brightened and work was more plentiful. Moreover on Castlereagh's death there was a Cabinet reshuffle which gave more influence to men who wanted something less sterile than mere repression and who were prepared to introduce gradual reforms in at least the economic sphere. Canning, who had been at the Board of Control from 1816 to 1820 – when he resigned over the ministerial decision to acquiesce in George IV's determination to put his wife, Queen Caroline, whom he detested, on trial on a charge of adultery – returned as Foreign Secretary. Peel, a moderate reformer, became Home Secretary, and Huskisson, an old friend of the Melbournes, went to the Board of Trade. Lord Grenville and his followers also decided to join the Government, reducing still more the Whig ranks. William, more from loyalty than conviction, felt that he must still stand by his old friends and associates, Lord Holland and Lord Grey, in spite of Canning's angling for him to accept office in 1824. Three years later he changed his mind. In 1827 Liverpool was incapacitated by a stroke and Canning was asked to head a new administration. His ambition and self-confidence had alienated many people; moreover the more die-hard Tories, Wellington, Peel and Eldon, suspected his policies and resigned. To replace them Canning turned to the idea of a coalition with at least some of the Whigs, a move made easier by the fact that he too favoured a policy of Roman Catholic emancipation which had long been a plank in the Whig platform. Lord Grey, who looked down on him as a plebeian, could not bring himself to serve under him, but William Lamb, who even when in opposition had found himself often in sympathy with the new Prime Minister's politics, was inhibited by no such prejudice and accepted his offer of the post of Chief Secretary for Ireland. There were some minor difficulties to be overcome. He was once again no longer a member of the Commons, having decided not to fight his seat at Hertford when opposed by a candidate who was very free with his money and equally ready to drag up William's matrimonial scandals and make capital out of them. In the election of 1825, however, a safe seat was found for him and his career as a politician had at last begun in earnest as a minister of the Crown.

The Irish Secretaryship did not carry with it a place in the Cabinet and it exiled him from Westminster, the seat of power; but for the first time in his life William had an opportunity of exercising authority and testing his own ability for administration. At last, at the age of forty-seven, he had something into which he could get his teeth. It also gave him an opportunity to familiarise himself with the Irish problem, though in 1827 he can hardly have guessed how important a part that country was to play in his subsequent career. In many ways, in sending him to Ireland Canning had served him well. In 1827 that country looked more like being a constant irritation than a major headache, and in such a situation Lamb could be relied upon never to aggravate it by hasty action or intolerant views. Essentially a middle-of-the-road man, if anyone could find common ground between warring factions and provide moderate solutions for dealing with crying evils, he could. Moreover he had one asset in that, like Canning, he sincerely believed in the necessity of Roman Catholic emancipation, partly because he was sceptic enough to deplore the persecution of people for differing on the details of anything so unsure as revealed religion, and partly because he felt that the time had come to satisfy a demand that, unsatisfied, might lead to still greater trouble.

About the existence of unrest, turbulence and violence in the country there could be no two opinions. For this there were two main causes, one political, one economic. Politically the Irish resented the Act of Union, which they knew their own ancient Parliament had been bribed and manoeuvred into accepting for the benefit of England not Ireland. It had left the Irish members in a permanent minority at Westminster and had burdened the Irish revenues with what turned out to be too heavy a load for the economy of the country to carry. As far as the Irish could see there was no safeguard for their interests. Had the Act of Union been followed by the removal of all the disabilities which still prevented the Catholic majority from exercising the full rights of citizenship they might have been more reconciled. But when no Catholic gentleman could rise higher in the army than the rank of colonel, to give but one example, and when a proposal to rectify this had even led to the fall of the Whig government in 1807, the Catholic gentry remained full of frustration. But the greatest grievance of all was their political impotence. In an attempt to placate Catholic feeling and extend to them some rights the younger Pitt had allowed them to vote for their Parliamentary representatives, but in 1827, as in 1793, they could only return Protestants. This meant that genuine Irish interests and genuine Irish opinion could never be defended and explained at Westminster while only the Protestant minority had a voice. The second fundamental problem, which affected even the poorest Irish peasant, to whom politics would normally have been a closed book, was the desperately low standard of living of the Irish people. In Ireland as in England there had been a population explosion; too many people were trying to live off too little land farmed by traditional methods which produced far too little to meet the growing demand for food that was made upon it. Absentee landlords, many of whom were Protestants living in England for most of the year – Lord Palmerston for instance had estates in Sligo which he perhaps visited twice annually – tended to perpetuate the abuses which menaced the living standards of the peasantry. Even when they did not do so by active and conscious exploitation of their estates, in the eyes of their tenants they were still held guilty. In fact most of the exploitation was the work of middlemen and agents who, because of the land hunger, were able to take advantage of the utterly insecure legal position of the tenantry. In many ways it was a vicious circle, too complicated to explain here, but the result was a mass of misery in the Irish countryside against which, because neither the law nor the authorities gave them any protection, the peasantry themselves reacted by cattle maiming, arson and murder. This was the Ireland which it now fell to William Lamb to administer in the name of His Majesty's Government.

His freedom of action was circumscribed by the fact that he was responsible to the Home Secretary at Westminster and that he had to work with the Duke of Wellington's touchy elder brother, Lord Wellesley, since 1821 Lord Lieutenant of Ireland. There was not therefore much that he could do in a constructive way, even if positive action had come more easily to him than it ever did. Moreover his term in Ireland proved to be a short one. Owing to the changing political circumstances that followed Canning's death in September 1827 Lamb was out of office by May 1828; when next he had to deal with Ireland's problems it was as Prime Minister. At least his stay in Dublin equipped him better than most Prime Ministers to understand the Irish. Much later he told Queen Victoria that in his opinion no solution provided by the British government would ever produce a settlement, because it was the Irish temperament rather than specific grievances that was responsible for the ever-recurring crises. But while he was in Ireland he at least took the trouble to meet every section of those Irishmen who moved in political and social circles. Earlier Chief Secretaries had held aloof from Roman Catholics, meeting familiarly only Protestants. Lamb made no distinction between them. He had possibly more in common with the easy, casual Catholic approach to life than with the Protestants who, as a dominant minority, tended to extreme religious views and a stricter code of behaviour. What he had thought earlier about the Scottish Dissenters might well have described his reactions to the Protestant Irish: 'They are more zealous and consequently more intolerant than the Established Church. Their only object is power. If we are to have a prevailing religion, let us have one that is cool and indifferent . . . Not that I am so foolish as to dread any fires and faggots and wheels and axes, but there are other modes of persecution. Toleration is the only good and just principle and toleration for every opinion that can possibly be form'd.' So wrote the Glasgow student and so the mature politician still felt. If anything his Dublin experience reinforced his views, views he was to hold all his life.

His door therefore was open to anyone who liked to take the trouble to approach him and he was as likely to grace Catholic as Protestant social occasions. Even his methods of doing business were more likely to please the Irish than the correct impersonal official attitude that so many Englishmen adopted. He never protected his official privacy behind a barrier of secretaries and protocol. The only order was 'Show him in' even when this resulted in a babel of sound. On one occasion he was driven to apologise for the incoherence of a letter he was penning to the Home Office with the excuse 'I have a dozen fellows talking to me whilst I write this letter.' All his life he was to conduct business in the same casual manner, even as Prime Minister seeing people in his bedroom and never hiding behind official jargon. True he often used his apparent lack of ceremony to avoid awkward issues with a joke or a neatly turned phrase but this he did with so much charm and courtesy that even a refusal, though it disappointed, did not leave a barb of resentment. The Irish will forgive much to the man who neither offends their dignity nor makes them feel inferior; Lamb did neither, though, because the patronage that he had to dispense was meagre in comparison with the hordes of people who came seeking it, refusals, however pleasantly worded, were far more common than opportunities to gratify a request.

In spite of his almost negligent public manner he was far from idle during these months in Ireland. He worked hard acquainting himself with the main Irish issues, the thorny land situation, the payment of tithes by a Catholic majority to support an alien minority church, and questions of abuses in local government. A steady flow of reports and memoranda to Westminster on these and kindred topics give the lie to his reputation for laziness but they also illustrate his lack of constructive thinking; like many politicians dealing with Ireland he found it easier to diagnose the ailment than to suggest a cure. The more he studied Ireland's problems the more he came to the conclusion that there was little that government could do. In taking this attitude he was not only illustrating his supreme mastery of the art of doing nothing and his own innate conviction that only too often the cure was worse than the disease in its final consequences; he was also acting in accordance with contemporary economic thinking. Ministers saw the function of government as preserving law and order, raising revenue and directing foreign policy; they believed themselves incapable of manipulating economic forces or engaging in what today might be described as social engineering. When the desperate cotton weavers had appealed to Lord Liverpool's government for help he had replied that, much as he sympathised with their distress, to attempt to interfere with economic laws could only make bad worse. With the disciples of *laissez faire* preaching such doctrines, Lamb had some excuse for confining his efforts to investigation. In any case the gulf between the desperate state of the peasantry and the life led by the gentry in Dublin was too great to be bridged, except possibly intellectually, in the time afforded to Lamb.

He was perhaps lucky in that no important political crisis arose while he was in charge of Irish affairs, because in 1827 a major one was already brewing. This was very largely due to a gifted Irishman, Daniel O'Connell, with whom later, when he became Lord Melbourne, Lamb was to have many dealings. O'Connell, like the would-be parliamentary reformers in England, had grasped the fact that political power was essential if economic and social grievances were ever to be redressed. To secure this it was essential that the Roman Catholic population must be directly represented in the House of Commons. The Liberator, as he came to be known, was revolutionary in his aims, but in his campaign he was careful to keep within the letter of the law. In 1823 he founded a Catholic League to which a year later he persuaded even the poorest Catholics to subscribe a penny a month. The authorities ordered the dissolution of the League as prejudicial to good order but O'Connell, who was a skilful lawyer, always managed to keep one move ahead of the law, and funds continued to roll in. In the year before Lamb came to Ireland the Irish leader began to use his organisation to secure the return of candidates prepared to support the Catholic aims, thus demonstrating that the Irish voter was capable of being marshalled effectively. By the time that O'Connell was ready to take the next step and to stand himself in a by-election in Clare, William Lamb had resigned. In was in 1829 that Wellington and Peel, who hitherto had stoutly opposed all arguments for Roman Catholic emancipation, realising that O'Connell's tactics could be repeated ad infinitum, to the intense embarrassment of the Ministry, yielded to necessity and once again admitted Roman Catholics to Parliament.

William's resignation from an office that he had enjoyed was yet another illustration of his loyalty to his friends and colleagues. Since Canning's death there had been no one of his stature to lead the party that he had created and, after a brief interim government under Lord Godrich, George IV once again asked the Duke of Wellington to form an administration. This left the Canningites, of whom the most important were Palmerston, Huskisson and William's old friend Ward, in a difficult position. They distrusted the Duke but thought they might be more effective in moderating his policies if they remained in office. In this they miscalculated. The Duke commanded his Cabinet as he had commanded his army and when there was disagreement as to how the members for two boroughs, East Redford and Penryn, which had been disenfranchised for corrupt practices, should be allotted, the fact that Huskisson felt he could not support the Government's decision in the House was to the Duke tantamount to mutiny. When, therefore, Huskisson wrote him a letter that could be, and in the heat of the moment probably was, intended to be one of resignation, Wellington promptly accepted it in spite of Palmerston's subsequent efforts to explain it away. If Huskisson went his friends felt that they must go with him, though personally Lamb considered the Duke's solution the more preferable. So by May 1828 Lamb was once again in opposition. He was never again to sit in the Commons as a minister of the Crown. In July his father died and William succeeded to the title and to his father's seat in the Lords. It was a welcome change. He had always disliked the rough and tumble of a contested election. Yet to stand for a safe borough was not often to his liking, not because he disapproved of the system but because he did not want to be bound to follow the politics of his patron, which in honour he would have felt obliged to do. A seat in the Lords freed him from either of these necessities. Also, though a witty and original conversationalist, he did not greatly enjoy speaking in the Commons; he preferred discussion and compromise behind the scenes. In the Lords he was under less pressure. There, casual as his manner often was, particularly when he did not want to show his hand, he could speak with fire and determination. On one occasion when Haydon, the painter, was listening to a debate on the Irish Church he described his astonishment when 'up starts Melbourne like an artillery rocket. He began in a fury. His language flowed out like fire; he made such palpable hits that he floored the Duke as if he had shot him. But the moment the situation was over, his habitual apathy got ahead, he stammered, hummed and hawed. It was the most pictorial exhibition of the night. He waved his white hand with all the natural grace of Talma, expanded his broad chest, looked right at his adversary like a handsome lion, and grappled him with the grace of Paris.'

Not only did William leave the Commons for the Lords, he made another break with the past; Melbourne House, with its traditions of lavish entertainment, was sold. Henceforth his London home was a more modest one, suitable for a bachelor establishment, in South Street, Mayfair. The period between his resignation in May 1828 and November 1830 was the last spell of leisure that he was to enjoy until his final retirement in 1841, but in 1828 he could hardly have expected that he would return, not only to office, but to a commanding position in a genuine Whig government.

5

HOME SECRETARY

IT was ironic that the growing demand throughout the country for parliamentary reform should have brought Melbourne back not only to office but to high office, because it was not something of which he approved. Nevertheless, though he was distinctly lukewarm towards the policy which the Whigs were now pledged to follow in this matter, he was glad to be back in office. The two years that had intervened between his resignation in 1828 and his appointment as Home Secretary in 1830 had been empty and unsatisfying when his life seemed to have no definite focus. Troubled though his marriage had been it had brought with it responsibilities that must have occupied much of his thoughts, even when these thoughts had not been pleasant ones. Moreover while his wife lived he was conscious of being needed, and a person who is needed can never experience complete loneliness. Indeed in the more peaceful interlude towards the end of Lady Caroline's life, when neither she nor his parliamentary duties were making any great demand on him, she was of the opinion that though in such circumstances he should have been the happiest of men, she doubted whether this was the case. In 1828 within a few months he had lost first his wife and then his employment. The result was to leave him aimless, something which he had too much zest for living ever to enjoy. He once confessed that he had never regretted the time he had spent in amusing himself, even when

70

his occupations had been foolish or wrong, but that he looked back with dissatisfaction on months and years spent in idleness, in sleeping and in sauntering as being 'as much without present pleasure as future fruit and advantage.' For a time he contemplated the idea of turning to authorship but found that the protracted discipline needed to write more than verse and articles was beyond him. The trouble was, he wrote, that he had 'read too much and too little, so that it has extinguished all the original fire of my genius, and yet not enough to furnish me with the power of writing words of mature thinking and solid instruction.' The rich treasures he had garnered in years of reading were better suited to adorn his conversations, since the possession of an excellent memory made them so easily available at the appropriate time. As Victoria was to discover later Melbourne was not only the most entertaining but also the most instructive of companions.

But in 1828 there was nobody to instruct. Lamb, as he still was, had taken his son, Augustus, with him to Ireland, perhaps with the hope that fresh scenes might strike some spark in his clouded mind, but it was clear, even to his father, that the young man was incapable of responding to the mental stimulus that a man like Melbourne could so gladly have provided for any normal son. In an age when less was known about the mentally and physically handicapped than is the case today Augustus's symptoms were neither widely known nor publicly discussed. Caroline writing to Godwin said of him 'my boy, though afflicted, is clever, amiable and cheerful' but other accounts indicate that he was mentally retarded and that he needed constant surveillance. It is a proof of Melbourne's deep affection for him that this was so frequently provided by his father, instead of his son being placed in the care of some suitable person and kept out of sight.

Deprived of the companionship of his son in this hiatus in his life, perhaps inevitably Melbourne turned to a woman for consolation. Female society had always been necessary to him. His links with his mother had been of the closest. After her death he declared 'My mother was a most remarkable woman; not merely clever and engaging, but the most sagacious woman I ever knew. She kept me right as long as she lived.' Next to his mother his love was given to his sister Emily, who, in the year of his own marriage, had married Lord Cowper and after his death took Lord Palmerston as her second husband in 1839. Melbourne's standards were high, particularly where older women were concerned. With younger ones his attitude was protective, almost paternal; it was to older, more mature women that he looked for understanding, for amusement and for intelligent conversation. He was almost a pre-ordained victim for charming, sophisticated, unhappy wives, two of whom came near to wrecking his public image. The first of these near-disastrous entanglements was with a Lady Brandon. While in Dublin he had seen a good deal of her; her husband, with whom she was on bad terms, was an Irish peer and a clergyman. Later in life and in another connection Melbourne's brother Frederick was to observe that William was habitually incautious, and he made no secret of the many evenings he spent in her company. When she removed to London the friendship continued until it was finally dragged into publicity by her husband, who for much of the time had been absent taking the waters at Buxton and who, if rumour was correct, seemed initially more concerned with any advantages that his wife's connection with Lord Melbourne might bring him rather than with the need to protect her virtue or his honour. When no such advantages seemed likely to materialise he brought an action against Melbourne on the grounds that Melbourne had been seen leaving his wife's house in the early hours of the morning. The judge dismissed such flimsy evidence with contempt; perhaps on this occasion Melbourne had shown more caution than his brother had thought him to possess. No evidence that more than a warm friendship existed between them has ever come to light; nevertheless some doubt must remain in view of the fact that he made Lady Brandon a quite substantial allowance for the rest of his life, an allowance that he asked his family should be continued after his death. When Frederick was trying to disentangle Melbourne's finances many years later he found that his brother was still financing her to the tune of some £800 to £1,000 a year. So perhaps he was lucky in that the case Lord Brandon brought against him was so summarily dismissed. Whether as that of a friend or of a mistress her companionship when he most needed it was something he valued for the rest of his life.

From 1830 Melbourne had more serious public matters with which to occupy himself. In that year parliamentary reform became an issue which all politicians had to face and on which they were forced to take a stand either for or against; it could no longer be avoided. Two quite unconnected events contributed to this situation. One was the death of George IV in June which, in accordance with constitutional practice, necessitated a general election. The other was a new revolution in France, as a result of which the Bourbons were driven out and replaced by Louis Philippe, who in popular eyes at least, represented a triumph for the bourgeois element in society. Both events gave an impetus to demands for reform of the British representative system as enshrined in the House of Commons, which had been under spasmodic attack since the late eighties of the previous century. Parliament was the product of British history and as such had mirrored the distribution of wealth and power within the community which it represented at any given time. In medieval England both the Crown and the baronage had struggled to dominate it, with victory going to the Crown by the sixteenth century. This victory was challenged by Parliament itself, and in particular by the Commons, by resort to civil war in the seventeenth century, as it struggled to win its own independence. By the eighteenth century a constitutional balance had been achieved between the King, as head of the executive, and Parliament, as the legislature, so that neither could fulfil its role in the constitutional running of the country unless a reasonable harmony could be maintained between them. This was the work of ministers who were responsible to both King and Parliament, which meant that only too often they found themselves between the devil and the deep blue sea. Though by 1830 the balance had tipped very much in favour of Parliament the King had still to be consulted and his opposition could make things difficult for ministers, while his dislike was still a serious impediment to any politician who incurred it. Because of this growing power of Parliament, and in particular that of the House of Commons through its control of taxation, it was becoming increasingly important for each section of the community with interests to protect to secure representation in the Lower House.

Logically the old system, if indeed it could ever be so described, could not be defended but empirically it had mirrored the distribution of wealth and power within the eighteenth century with considerable realism. Basically

Parliament, and this was true of both Lords and Commons, represented the Landed Interest and the Anglican Church. In the case of the Commons this was not only, or even chiefly, because an act of 1710 had imposed a property qualification for members, namely land to the annual value of £600 for a knight of the shire and £300 for a member representing a borough, but because of the nature of the franchise. In the counties this had, at least, the virtue of uniformity; the right to vote was confined to the forty shilling freeholder. In the boroughs there was no such uniformity. Borough charters had been granted at different times and in different circumstances and followed not one but a number of patterns in determining the right of the inhabitants to vote. In a limited number of boroughs the franchise was wide enough to allow every male householder to vote but such boroughs, commonly known as potwalloper boroughs, were in the minority. In some the right to vote was restricted to the freemen, in others to those who paid certain ancient rates known as scot and lot, in still others to the owners of certain tenements within the borough, known as burgage tenure. In these types of boroughs the number of voters was manageably small. Two thirds had an electoral roll of less than 500, while in some of them there were less than a score of voters. Yet each borough returned two members. Such constituencies were particularly open to the influence which an important landowner could exert over them, so that in the political parlance of the day they were described as 'pocket boroughs' whose voters could be relied upon to return unopposed any man nominated by the patron of the borough. Only when the number of electors was too large to be managed in this way, or when families or groups of families were fighting to control a borough in which they both had an interest, was there likely to be a contested election with all the canvassing and beer and bribery that this involved and which Lamb had found so distasteful. The result was to secure a near monopoly of seats in the Commons for the landed gentry and the great aristocratic families, the heads of which already had a hereditary seat in the Lords. Politics were still the preserve of gentlemen, though the wealthy merchant or financier found little difficulty in obtaining the requisite influence in some borough, not infrequently by the purchase of an estate. This was the way in which the merely wealthy infiltrated the ranks of the gentry, as had the first Mathew Lamb.

Nevertheless to nurse a borough was a delicate and expensive business; the relations between a patron and his borough have been compared to those between a man and his mistress; to retain one's hold needed both wariness and money. As a result, when a nomination was not required for an eldest son or near relation or close friend, boroughs were in the market, it being understood that the borough owner would be well recompensed for his nomination. Because of the extensive patronage at its disposal in the Government, the Church, the Law and the armed services, the Ministry of the day was in a strong position to secure the election of members well disposed towards it in return for favours shown to the borough-mongers. It was this judicious exchange of favours between the great families who controlled the boroughs and the Government that enabled the latter to secure a solid body of supporters in the Commons. Today such practices would be considered corrupt; in the eighteenth century they were regarded as part of the normal machinery of government, and one reason why Melbourne and men who thought as he did were apprehensive about the consequences of parliamentary reform was that without this use of patronage it would be impossible to provide enough solid support for the ministry. At a period when party organisation was not strong enough to prevent members from becoming a disintegrated horde of individuals patronage provided the necessary cohesive factor. For this reason alone the distribution of patronage in the form of places and pensions was one of the most delicate and invidious tasks that ministers had to perform, as Melbourne discovered when he held the Irish Secretaryship. His experience was that for fifty persons seeking favours forty nine had to be disappointed. His own political career, if it is to be judged fairly, must be judged against this background. He and his contemporaries took it for granted that for a man to become a member of the Commons he must either be wealthy enough to buy a seat or have an 'interest' with the patron of a borough, and that this patron must be roughly of his own political opinions; a man of honour could not accept a nomination and then vote consistently against the views of his patron. This was one reason why Lamb refused Lord Holland's offer of a seat in 1815; close though the friendship between the two men was he found himself increasingly out of sympathy with the outlook of the Foxite Whigs. On the other hand, though he was no longer in the House when Canning offered him the Irish Secretaryship there was no difficulty in finding him a safe seat once he had accepted. In the absence of 'interest' or where an election was fought out between two rival interests, to stand as a candidate in a contested election could be extremely costly. It was lack of money that decided William Lamb not to stand in the election of 1812.

In a country that derived the greater part of its wealth from the land and its products, to concentrate political power in the hands of the men who were either landowners or connected with them did not seem unreasonable to a generation who had no conception of equality. This was the accepted pattern of politics and the standpoint from which the ruling groups of a traditionally hierarchic society viewed the demand that this power should be widely shared; how widely was a matter of dispute even among the reformers themselves. But by 1830 even the defenders of the status quo were beginning to realise that the England in which they had been born was altering with every decade; industry was employing more and more people, more and more of whom were living in towns. The population of the country as a whole was exploding; roughly speaking within Melbourne's life it doubled. Not only were more people employed in new ways, the structure of society was itself changing. Though the profits of agriculture had originally produced a pool of capital within the country, new cotton mills were producing an ever increasing amount, much of it invested in industry and communications. Husskinson, a notoriously accident-prone man, managed to get himself killed at the official opening of the Liverpool to Manchester railway. Men who designed mills and railways, men who financed them, men who managed them, men who ran the shops that catered for the new wealth, lawyers and doctors and teachers, were now numerous enough and sufficiently well-off to be recognised as the 'middle classes'. Beneath them the mass of the working population, once known as the 'labouring poor', was also changing in character as the opportunities and variety of employment grew. Among them were many forceful, clever and skilful men with a passion for education. These new working classes were quite capable of throwing up their own leaders, though admittedly many of these, like Francis Place the famous tailor of Charing Cross, who once had to dun Melbourne himself for an overdue account, came from the ranks of the skilled London craftsmen. Both the middle class and the new type of working class had interests for which to fight, interests that frequently clashed with those of the landowners. Cheap food was only one of these. A series of Corn Laws which, at least in theory, favoured the corn grower at the expense of the bread eater, were bitterly resented in overcrowded industrial towns. Many new manufacturers argued that Free Trade was essential for their interests. For much of the century life for working folk, in town and country alike, had been hard, with high prices and fluctuating employment as, during the post-war period, Britain had staggered from one economic crisis to another. Much of what had happened was in fact beyond the power of any government to control, even if the economic theories of the day had encouraged the attempt, but then, as now, people suffering hardship and distress blamed the Government and argued that, had they been able to bring political pressure to bear, their sufferings would have been remedied. One such leader, William Cobbett, went so far as to proclaim in his working class paper, 'The Political Register', after drawing a moving picture of the plight of the agricultural labourer 'shivering with an unshaven face and a carcass half covered with a ragged smock', that political reform was the answer to all these evils.

Reform to be effective would necessitate drastic changes in both the franchise and the distribution of seats. Boroughs had obtained the right to send members to Parliament when very different economic conditions had prevailed: when for instance the north and the midlands were backward areas, when Birmingham had been only a small town and Manchester a mere manor. Whether a town returned members or not depended on the accidents of history and its medieval or sixteenth centry importance; Bristol, Liverpool and Preston were represented, Manchester and Birmingham were not. The shift of industry from the south and west to the north and midlands had by 1830 made nonsense of the old distribution of seats. In the same way changes in the class structure made it necessary to have some common denominator in the borough franchise so that men in a roughly equal social and economic position should enjoy the same measure of representation. In 1830 an artisan in a constituency with a wide franchise had a vote, while in a neighbouring pocket borough a substantial businessman might quite well have none. This was the problem for which the Whigs had to find some acceptable solution, acceptable both to themselves and to reformers.

Today, when universal suffrage is considered to be almost a fundamental human right there is a hindsight tendency to concentrate sympathy on the men who fought, often gallantly and at considerable risk and hardship to themselves, for parliamentary reform in the thirties. Less sympathy and understanding has been shown to those who, like Wellington, opposed it outright, or who, like Melbourne and Palmerston, very slowly and with considerable misgivings came to regard it as a disagreeable necessity. As the former declared during a debate in the Lords on the Second Reform Bill, 'If there ever was an individual in the country more anxious than another that the affairs of the country might have gone on without being forced to incur the hazard and responsibility which must result from so great and a fundamental change in the House of Commons I am that person.' Nevertheless by 1830 Melbourne had come to the conclusion that the demand for reform was now both widespread and deep-rooted, much as he continued to doubt its wisdom. Meeting the diehards' argument that the popular clamour for this reform only appeared in bad times and subsided when they improved he went on, 'When Your Lordships see on every occasion of public calamity and distress, from whatever cause arising, the people call for an alteration in the representation and that call is accompanied with a deep rankling sense of injustice and of rights withheld, can Your Lordships suppose that an opinion so continually revived has not some deep seated foundation, and can you be insensible to the dangers of continuing a permanent cause for angry and discontented feelings to be revived and renewed at every period of public distress and calamity?' In this argument lay the key to much of his political philosophy. Change for its own sake he never sought, and indeed actively shunned; partly through inate conservatism (William IV described him as 'a Conservative in the truest sense of the word'); partly due to natural indolence, though he could be diligent enough in doing something that he thought must be done; and partly, indeed perhaps chiefly, because he believed that the good which men planned and looked for rarely rewarded their well meant efforts. Nevertheless though he believed that the mass of public opinion was usually wrong he believed even more strongly, as he told the Lords, that 'Although it might be our duty to resist the will of the people for a time, is it possible to resist it for ever?' To him the duty of the politician was to judge when that moment had come and then to decide how much must be conceded. In these two tenets lay much of his wisdom. To give too little too late was always a political blunder and one to which he attributed much of the trouble in Ireland. As he said ruefully, when speaking of that country, 'It is too bad that when the right thing is done it was done so tardily and insincerely as to falsify every reasonable anticipation, and to realise every evil augury. What all the wise men promised has not happened; and what all the damned fools said would happen has come to pass.'

The Whig party in general were more committed to reform than enthusiastic about it when they took office in 1830. In the late eighteenth centry they had been advocating the idea for reasons very different from those that were animating the parliamentary reformers of the nineteenth century. Charles James Fox, their leader, had been intensely disliked by George III, and none of the politicians leading the Whig groups in Parliament were particularly liked by him. The result was that only when circumstances were too strong for him would George III bow to the necessity of employing Whigs and while he could rely on a minister like Lord North or the younger Pitt to manage the business of the country to the general satisfaction of the Commons the ministerial control of patronage prevented the Whigs from gaining a majority in that House which could force the royal hand. When therefore the eighteenth centry Whigs spoke of parliamentary reform they meant measures that would lessen the control of the Crown over the pocket boroughs. The Whigs therefore, though pledged to some degree of reform, envisaged one that would strengthen the aristocratic not the popular control of the Commons. Nevertheless, because they were associated in men's minds with a programme of reform, men with very different and much more radical aims marched under their banner. In the general election of 1830 Whigs and men of more radical views increased their majority and when the Prime Minister, the Duke of Wellington, made it clear that in his opinion the existing system of representation was as near perfect as human wisdom could make it the fight was on. Melbourne considered such an outright gesture of defiance was a mistake. When a friend describing the Duke's action said 'He has thrown away the scabbard' Melbourne made the characteristic reply 'No, the sword with which he might have parried attack, and maintained the position for a good while.' The House expressed its dissatisfaction by defeating the ministry by 29 votes on a motion to reduce the Civil List and Wellington resigned. Lord Grey, the elderly and by no means enthusiastic reformer despite his close connection with the eighteenth century movement, now, after twenty years in opposition, found himself called upon to form a government. People in general, even in political circles, were surprised when he invited Melbourne to be his Home Secretary, partly because of his very limited experience of office, and partly because of his reputation as a dilettante, 'the once gay and still handsome Lord Melbourne'. Circumstances were, however, in his favour. The hard core of the Whigs had been in the political wilderness so long that experienced men to place in office were in short supply. Moreover Melbourne had done well in Ireland, and though he had joined Canning's government, which the aristocratic Lord Grey had refused to do, his social links with Holland and with Lord Grey himself had continued unbroken. But perhaps his greatest recommendation was his equanimity and his loyalty. With men as diverse as the radical Lord Durham and Lord Brougham the Chancellor on the progressive side, Grey realised the advantages of having a Home Secretary on whom he could rely to work smoothly with his colleagues and never to intrigue or stir up trouble.

In the actual framing of the reform bills Melbourne took a less active part than his more committed colleagues, though in Cabinet discussions he showed his usual combination of realism and conservatism in arguing that the urban franchise should be conferred on the £10 annual ratable value rather than on the higher figure of £20 combined with a ballot. Throughout his political career this issue of the use of a secret ballot in parliamentary elections remained a troublesome one, the radicals pushing for it and men like Melbourne fighting a rearguard action to preserve the traditional publicity of the hustings. It was a characteristic choice; he preferred the larger concession with its more popular appeal but with the safeguard that men should not be able to evade responsibility for their choice through the protection of the ballot box. On a later occasion he declared that 'The people as well as kings and ministers, are responsible to God . . . for the exercise of power committed to their charge', and the open casting of votes was one way of ensuring that this responsibility was publicly accepted. (It is an interesting speculation as to what would happen to the division lists in the modern House of Commons if MPs could avail themselves of the anonymity of the ballot box.) During these critical months Melbourne took his full share in cabinet discussions and argued strongly in the Lords in favour of the proposed measures, but his main energies were largely concentrated on the necessity of controlling a country that seemed almost on the brink of social revolution. Grain riots were not new in England – rioting when prices were high had been endemic in the eighteenth century – but the riots that occurred in the second and third decades of the nineteenth century were on such a scale as almost to merit the label 'revolt'. There had been serious riots in East Anglia in 1816 but in 1830 organised riots on a large scale spread with alarming rapidity throughout the southern rural counties in protest against the plight of the agricultural labourers. The causes of their distress were complex and arose out of changes in both the economic and social structure of the countryside. Agricultural workers and their families had become more dependent on wages as their main source of income just at the time when the price of food was rising sharply. Believing this to be a temporary emergency the local authorities had attempted to meet it by what was in effect a combination of a family allowance for larger families and a cost of living bonus, the standard admittedly being one of mere subsistence, known as the Speenhamland system. Unfortunately the emergency was not short-lived and the result was that wages were kept artificially low and the majority of agricultural labouring families were semi-pauperised from the cradle to the grave. The results were serious both for them and for the ratepayers. How far the demoralisation that this caused had spread is difficult to know and has been much debated. In the industrial parts of England the situation was less desperate; because there was alternative employment in the nearby towns farmers had to pay something approaching a more competitive wage. But in those counties that concentrated on the growing of grain families had to accept whatever wages were offered, or live on the parish or face an uprooting to go elsewhere in search of work. In 1816 the Board of Agriculture reported that one out of every three or four rural workers was unemployed and that wages were sometimes, though not invariably, from 15s to 9s a week. This was the situation which had resulted in the wide-scale rioting in East Anglia. In 1830 the trouble was still more extensive. In 1828 the harvest had been poor but at least the winter had been a mild one. The Harvest of 1829 had been even worse. Some of the grain remained unharvested until October and by then the snow was already lying on the ground. The memory of the cold, hunger and unemployment of that year was very fresh in men's minds in 1830, when both in France and in the English towns, where the reformers were active, there was a smell of revolution in the air.

For many labourers the final blow was the appearance of the threshing machine. Threshing had always been a standby winter employment and to cut the size of the labour force required and the hours of those normally so employed was to threaten what was already a deplorable standard of living. The number of machines actually to be found on the farms does not appear to have been great but the threat, and with it the fear, was there. In August 1830 the first threshing machines were destroyed in Kent and the infection rapidly spread through Berkshire, Buckinghamshire, Hampshire, Wiltshire and Dorset. The pattern everywhere was much the same. There was machine-breaking and arson, and in all the affected areas large crowds of countryfolk, women as well as men, gathered, going the rounds of the more substantial people's houses demanding contributions sometimes in money, sometimes merely refreshment, and always coupling their demands with one for better wages. Such demonstrations, though alarming to isolated gentry and the justices, were in the main remarkably restrained. Rarely did the rioters indulge in physical violence against persons, though property occasionally suffered, and in the aftermath there were no convictions for murder. Nevertheless the authorities were seriously alarmed, the more so because they viewed the riots as a concerted effort organised by a mysterious Captain Swing instead of being the result of an almost spontaneous combustion caused by contagious misery and distress.

This was the situation which faced Lord Melbourne when he

became Home Secretary. Tolerant though he was on many issues he invariably stood firm on the necessity of preserving law and order, which he considered to be one of the chief duties appertaining to government. In a speech which he made in the Commons on 2 January 1816 his point of view is clearly put. When, he said, assemblies led to breaches of the peace, he was for vigorous and immediate repression. This conduct he would recommend not only from motives of public security; but from motives of tenderness and mercy to the deluded persons themselves. He deprecated all breaches of the peace, disturbances and riots, not only for their immediate effects, but for their ultimate consequences. Tumult for liberty and right was not only dangerous and destructive, it was a liar and never kept its promises. Holding such views, despite his reputation for procrastination, he acted promptly, issuing the very day after he became Home Secretary a proclamation fixing a reward of £500 to anyone bringing incendiaries and rioters to justice. He next turned to the magistrates, who were still the linchpin of local official policy, to galvanise them into action, urging them to adopt a plan already sponsored by the Duke of Richmond for enrolling a volunteer force made up of small property holders, shopkeepers, yeomen and the like, and even 'respectable' labourers, to deal with local disorders. In addition to encouraging local authorities to show more vigour, officers were sent to the most disaffected districts to advise on the levying of volunteers and on the disposal of such troops as were available. Though Peel had instituted a metropolitan professional police force, outside the capital the military had to be called in when the situation got too serious to be dealt with by parish constables and magistrates. Nevertheless it was on the magistrates that the chief responsibility rested and in December Melbourne was again circularising them exhorting them not to give way to demands backed up by violence and reminding them that it was their duty to protect property of every description. Against sketchily armed and ill-led mobs such tactics were effective, or seemed to be. In fact the offer of better wages, even if made under duress, combined with the difficulty of organising anything but local demonstrations, which tended to splutter out once their initial impetus had been spent, may well have had as much to do with the collapse of agrarian protest as had Melbourne's sternness.

The aftermath was severe and Melbourne did nothing to mitigate it. A special commission was despatched to the affected counties to supplement the ordinary assize courts. Of all the cases tried 374 were dismissed, 252 were given prison sentences, 35 were ordered to be transported and 227 were sentenced to death. In the eighteenth and nineteenth centuries, when hanging was the penalty for many even minor offences (hence the proverb 'As well be hanged for a sheep as a lamb') the sentence was more usually commuted. Of the 252 prisoners convicted either by the special commissioners, who tended to be more lenient, or the regular judges of assize, only 19 were finally hanged, the majority having their sentences commuted to transportation for varying terms. In the judgement of his contemporaries Melbourne had done his work well and it is only fair to judge a man by the standards of his time, however repugnant they may be to future generations. There is little, however, to suggest that he found his task distasteful, which is interesting in view of the fact that as a young MP he had supported Romilly's attempts to abolish the death penalty for certain offences. Though when dealing with individual cases of hardship and injustice, particularly when they concerned people of his own world, he could be almost emotionally sentimental, he seems in general to have had very little of what today would be described as 'a social conscience'. Possibly this was because his imagination was limited by his intellect, and the lot of persons so far removed from his own way of life was beyond its range. Lady Caroline once told Lady Morgan that when a child she divided the world into dukes and beggars, and though to ascribe such views to Melbourne would be ridiculous he does seem to have been oblivious to those social problems that lay outside his immediate experience.

This negative quality he was to show again in dealing with the Dorchester labourers, the Tolpuddle Martyrs, in 1834. The nineteenth century had seen increasing activity on the part of the industrial workers to combine to secure better wages or shorter hours, a move that had alarmed the Government at a time when the dangerous doctrines of the French revolutionaries had seemed to challenge the British social order. As a result between 1799 and 1824 even to belong to one of these 'combinations' was made illegal and punishable by imprisonment. In 1824 the law had been modified and, though most of

William Lamb at the age of seventeen, painted by Hoppner.

The town and country houses in which William Lamb grew up:
(above) Brocket Hall, Hertfordshire, engraved by Fittler after Burney in 1786;
(below) Melbourne House in Whitehall, engraved in 1797 by T. Molton.

ABOVE Emily Lamb, William's sister, painted by Sir Thomas Lawrence in 1803. She married first Lord Cowper and then Lord Palmerston.

BELOW Lady Caroline Lamb engraved by Henry Meyer in 1819, and William Lamb engraved by S. Freeman after the portrait by Sir Thomas Lawrence.

Drawings made by Caroline Lamb in her sketchbook: (*above*) William and Caroline with their son Augustus; (*opposite*) Augustus.

ABOVE Caroline on her sickbed. This illustration has written beside it:
'*Sure means to make the mind and body part,*
A burning fever and a broken heart.'

A lithograph of Caroline Norton who was Melbourne's close friend from 1830 to his death.

ABOVE The House of Commons in 1821 by Pugin, Stephanoff and Bowyer. William Lamb is second from right in the second row up of the opposition benches.

BELOW Queen Victoria riding between Melbourne and his brother-in-law Palmerston in 1837. The lithograph, entitled 'Susannah and the Elders' is by John Doyle.

ABOVE In this cartoon of 14 January 1838, Queen Victoria is balanced on a seesaw, supported by John Bull, and she indicates her preference for the Whigs as Melbourne rises and Wellington sinks.

BELOW Melbourne signifies his approval of Queen Victoria's decision to marry Prince Albert while her uncle, the Duke of Cambridge, chides his son George for failing to win her hand.

the steps that such combinations could use to further their ends were still illegal, it was no longer a punishable offence to be a member. In the ferment of ideas generated by the struggle for the Reform Bill, combined with a mixture of circumstances and the heady socialist doctrines of Robert Owen, this Trade Union movement, as it was coming to be called, was especially active while Melbourne was at the Home Office. He disliked it but felt that unless the unions transgressed the limits imposed upon them by law there was nothing he could do. Also he was apprehensive lest 'an evil which has so long afflicted the manufacturing districts should not, in the present state of general restlessness, creep into and infect the agricultural areas'. By 1834 this was happening and in the Dorset village of Tolpuddle a group of labourers attempting to form a union fell foul of the law by swearing an oath, a practice that the panic legislation of 1797 had made illegal. Melbourne acted swiftly. The unfortunate and inoffensive men were tried, convicted and transported to Australia as an example before their fellow unionists and friends could organise petitions on their behalf. When Robert Owen organised a monster meeting at White Conduit Fields with the intention of presenting a petition for their release he was informed that Melbourne would only receive it if it was presented in a suitable manner by a small deputation. Owen agreed to present it by a deputation of only five but when Melbourne knew that the official deputation was to be accompanied by the whole body of demonstrators he calmly allowed himself to be seen at a front window and then dispatched his Under-Secretary with a message to the effect that he would not receive a petition so escorted, but that if they wished to bring it back on another occasion 'suitably presented' he would receive it. Rather surprisingly after this rebuff the crowd dispersed but their restraint availed them nothing. In spite of the considerable pressure of public opinion brought to bear on him Melbourne refused to recommend a pardon for the Tolpuddle Martyrs. Between him and the mass of the working class there was no rapprochement. Perhaps he spent too little of his adult life at Brocket to understand even remotely the heart of rural England; he preferred the birds and beasts of the countryside to its inhabitants, the cawing of the rooks to the sounds of human distress.

He had equally little sympathy with what was happening in

industrial areas where the new working classes were fighting for parliamentary rights because they had become convinced that without representation in the Commons they could never defend their own interests against the employers. Though unions were no longer illegal organisations any attempt on the part of workers to fight for more wages or shorter hours was still highly suspect as likely to produce disorder. Melbourne disliked and distrusted the unions as a potential danger to the public peace and as centres of dissatisfaction, a dislike accentuated during 1833 and 1834 by dramatic displays of union activity under the inspiration of Robert Owen. These were the years of the grandiose schemes for a Grand National Consolidated Trades Union, the years of strikes and lockouts. Nevertheless he refused to take panic action, turning down any suggestions for employing an *agent provocateur*. There was to be no repetition of the scandals of Oliver the Spy while he was Home Secretary; so long as the unions observed the limits of the law so would he. If they went beyond them he was prepared to back up the magistrates with exhortations to be firm in the face of disorder, and with troops when the Bench thought their assistance necessary. Privately he attributed much of the unrest in the industrial north to magistrates who failed to act with the necessary firmness. This was something he could not understand. In a letter to Lord Derby he attributed it partly to the lingering effects of Peterloo on the Bench but he was clearly worried about the efficiency of the magistrates, considering them far too eager to ask for troops and far from resolute in handling disturbances in their early stages. But though he disliked trade unionism he thought it something of a flash in the pan, a movement that had no future. By the end of 1834 all their hopeful schemes had collapsed and Melbourne argued that the British working man was at heart a sensible being and that the lesson he would draw from this failure was that the benefits for which the unions fought were illusory and that the loss of wages that strikes caused would convince him that the game was not worth the candle. It was a less unreasonable forecast in 1834 than historians, blessed with hindsight, sometimes concede.

During the first two years at the Home Office the threat to law and order was largely connected with the critical debates on the Reform Bill, particularly in the Lords, which Melbourne realised might produce a crop of demonstrations and even riots.

Preferring rather to prevent trouble than to deal with it Melbourne did his best to exercise a moderating influence behind the scenes. Through his secretary Tom Young, who in contemporary assessments was not quite a gentleman, he had connections with Francis Place, one of the leading radicals who was organising a monster petition to the King after the Lords had thrown out the Second Reform Bill. Place refused to give up the project but told Melbourne that 'the whole would be conducted in an orderly discreet way, so that no one need fear any disagreeable results', while at the same time advising him that it would be tactful to keep the police and the troops well out of sight. In Birmingham, where the Political Union planned to hold a great rally, to which its supporters were instructed to come armed, with the intention of pledging themselves to pay no taxes until the Reform Bill had been passed, Melbourne was more successful. Working through Place and his friends he contrived to get this potentially dangerous assembly indefinitely postponed. In Bristol he was less fortunate. The arrival of Sir Charles Wetherell, who had been Attorney General in Wellington's government and was also Recorder of Bristol, on 29 October for the business of gaol delivery, and the fact that he had voted consistently against the Bill in the Commons, was enough to spark off a riot. On this occasion Melbourne's doubts about the adequacy of the local Bench were fully justified. For three days the city was in the hands of the mob and 110 persons were killed, wounded or otherwise injured. The riots at Bristol during the agitation for the Reform Bill were the most serious but they were not unique. At Derby the rioters attacked the gaol; at Nottingham the old castle was burnt down. Melbourne was apprehensive of similar riots taking place in London. He felt confident that he could protect Westminster and its environs and he considered that the City was capable of looking after itself, but the large sprawling area of metropolitan London was frighteningly vulnerable. The Times advocated that law-abiding reformers should be organised as a voluntary constabulary but such a course was not without its own dangers. Such associations might be taken over by the extimists if the Reform Bill were to be rejected a third time while if the local associations should coalesce into one national union they would be a formidable force that might itself be used against authority. It was to guard against this that Melbourne issued a

proclamation on 21 November forbidding any such amal-
gamation. In the event this last emergency did not arise. On 3
June 1832 the bill passed its third reading in the Lords. This
result was not achieved without much argument in the Cabinet,
where the point at issue had been whether, and at what point, to
press the King to create enough new peers to over-ride the
anti-reformers in the Lords. Here again Melbourne followed a
cool realistic course, delaying until the last moment in the hope,
which proved well-founded, that after protracted negotiation
wiser councils would prevail and the dissident peers, by
refraining from voting, would allow the bill to pass.

Melbourne's four years as Home Secretary had been a
valuable and educative experience. Though familiar with the
world of politics since childhood, in spite of his short spell in
office in Ireland he had never been at the centre of power. Most
of his political life had been spent in opposition and things look
very different from the government benches. As an important
member of the Cabinet he could study for the first time all the
stresses and strains of conflicting policies and difficult
personalities. When Lord Durham was battling to carry radical
policies against his aging and conservative Prime Minister such
was his violence that Melbourne confessed that had he been in
Grey's position he would have knocked him down. Personally
he had no ambition to be Prime Minister, nor did he think it
likely. His present responsibilities were enough. It was not as if
he had any definite policies to advocate, or any personal
ambition to fulfil. Later he told Queen Victoria that if he had
his time to live over again he would have given himself up to a
life of ease and amusement and never have embarked on a
political career. When he made this statement he was aging and
weary and the double role of best friend to an exacting young
woman and running a difficult team was slowly wearing him
down, and should not be taken quite at its face value;
nevertheless it is a revealing remark.

6

PRIME MINISTER

In the June of 1834, to his own surprise and to that of every-body else, Lord Melbourne found himself First Lord of the Treasury. It was a political prize he had neither desired nor expected. One evening while as Home Secretary he had been dining with the fascinating and charming Mrs Norton, whose friendship was later to place him in a very awkward and equivocal position, he met a young friend of hers, Benjamin Disraeli, whose conversation amused and stimulated him. In the course of the evening he asked the young man about his future plans and ambitions and was told that these were to become Prime Minister. Melbourne did not, as so many Home Secretaries might have done, cut his young acquaintance down to size. Instead he was prepared to hold out to him the hope that he might very well carve out for himself a political career, but as far as becoming Prime Minister was concerned Melbourne assured him 'No chance of that in our time', continuing that Grey 'will certainly be succeeded by one who has a requisite for the position, in the prime of life and fame, of old blood, high rank, great fortune and greater ability. Once in power there is nothing to prevent him holding office as long as Sir Robert Walpole. Stanley will be the next Prime Minister, you will see'. The Hon. Edward Stanley had quickly made his mark in Melbourne's old office as Secretary for Ireland. His brilliance in debate was undoubted, earning him the nickname of 'the Rupert of debate' and he had the vigour and self-confidence, amounting to sheer arrogance, that was able to impose itself on the hesitant and the doubtful. Though, as in Melbourne's day, the Irish Secretaryship was intended to be an office subordinate to the general policy laid down by the Home Secretary, in June 1831 he was admitted to the Cabinet and henceforth by the force of his own personality it was Stanley who imposed his solutions on it rather than the reverse. Yet ironically it was Stanley's own handling of the Irish question that led to Melbourne being asked to form a government in July 1834.

There had been no particular reason why Melbourne's first office should have been the Irish Secretaryship but for the rest of his official life Ireland could never be left out of his calculations: for much of his premiership he had to depend on the Irish vote. Some understanding therefore of the state of Irish politics is necessary because of their impact on the Whig party and on Melbourne's own parliamentary position. It was the generalship of Daniel O'Connell that had finally wrung Roman Catholic emancipation from the Tory government of Wellington and Peel and in 1830 the Liberator had taken his seat in the Commons, where in his green coat and black wig he became a notable figure. He was also the leader of a sizeable contingent, and as such was of vital importance to Lord Grey's reform ministry. The second reading of the First Reform Bill, which was only carried by one vote, would not have been carried at all had it not been for the Irish vote. Even though the general election of 1831, which had followed its final rejection, had greatly increased the strength of the reformers in the House, throughout all the subsequent struggle the support of the Irish members continued to be of great importance. Nevertheless O'Connell and his Irish supporters were embarrassing allies. Irishmen were not popular in England, partly because the old prejudice against Roman Catholicism was still strong and it was feared that to give them complete control, or even to increase their existing control, over Irish affairs would be dangerous to Protestant interests. As a result of this fear the act for their emancipation had not brought the expected enlargement of their activities to the Catholic Irish. It is true that the law now accorded them the same legal status as Protestants but, in an age when patronage was the accepted oil for the lubrication of government, posts continued to be given to Protestants not to

Catholics. O'Connell himself was a victim. As an outstanding member of the Irish Bar he had a claim to high legal office, yet he was not even promoted to be a King's Counsel until political pressure forced the hands of his nominal allies, the Whigs. By 1832 therefore, finding the support he and his friends had given to Grey's government so shabbily rewarded, he began to advocate the repeal of the Union between the two countries, an idea to which all the English parties were completely opposed.

Nevertheless, as a ministry pledged to reform and cumbered with Radical allies sympathetic to the Irish cause, the administration had to make some show of dealing with Irish grievances, even if they dared not gratify O'Connell's ambition. In Ireland, as in England at that date, there were basically two nations, the gentry, whether Catholic or Protestant, and the peasantry who were almost entirely Catholic and whose problems were social and economic rather than political. These were complex and can only be briefly indicated. As in England the population was growing rapidly; Irish industry was not sufficiently developed to absorb these increasing numbers and the Irish economy remained therefore largely agricultural. The result was a chronic land shortage, with holdings subdivided and let at exaggerated rents because of the competition for every scrap of land however poor. Absentee landlordism was another factor, so was the creation of sub-tenancies and a law that made evictions easy and denied compensation to tenants for any improvement that they might have made. Moreover improvements in farming methods merely instituted a vicious circle, because until farms were consolidated these were not possible and yet if consolidation took place where were the evicted peasants to go? The peasantry, burdened with excessive rents and a tithe payable to an alien church, in addition to contributions made to their own priests, were in a state of desperation. Peasants, whether evicted for non-payment of rent, or distrained upon for non-payment of tithes, shot at agents and maltreated, even murdered, other peasants who had taken over their smallholdings. By 1830 in part of the south-east violence and outrage of every kind were being resorted to in a resolute determination not to pay the hated tithe.

Melbourne had considerable instinctive sympathy with Roman Catholic grievances though, as the years went by, he became increasingly convinced that the removal of specific ones

91

would do little to assuage Irish hostility, which he thought was rooted not in their wrongs but in their temperament. Nevertheless he recognised that for political reasons remedies must be sought, however much he doubted their efficacy. Even then, from the time of his sojourn in Dublin, he believed in proceeding step by step, writing to Rice, the Under-Secretary, 'Let one measure be adopted and settle down a little before you bring in another. If you dash at the whole at once you run the risk of producing confusion and discrediting your reforms.' The initial problem facing Lord Grey's ministry was to decide which reforms to introduce since basically what was acceptable to O'Connell and the Irish was not acceptable to the English Parliament. O'Connell wanted Repeal, which would have put Ireland in charge of her own destiny, and the complete abolition of tithe, which would have robbed the Anglican church in Ireland of a major part of its revenue. On the demand for Repeal Melbourne was adamant, insisting that it must be made crystal clear to the Irish people that this was something that no efforts of theirs could ever secure. He was equally against trying to placate O'Connell by coming to some arrangement with him, arguing that no British government could pay his price, which was high office, warning that 'the Ministry that lets him get into the saddle may be very sure that he will soon have a bit in their mouths and guide them as he lists'. But though personally opposed to O'Connell, who was heartily disliked in the Commons because of what was described as 'the low scurrility of his speeches' which produced 'a general conviction that he is an irreclaimable blackguard and that it is unfit for any gentleman to associate with him', he remained conscious of the anomalous position of the Anglican Church in Ireland. Its membership of some 800,000 was a mere drop in the ocean of the 6,000,000 or so Roman Catholics, who nevertheless had to pay tithe for its upkeep. Melbourne was prepared therefore to act with the more liberal members in the Cabinet, little doctrinaire Lord John Russell, Lord Althorp and Lord Durham, in attempting to reorganise the Church and to divert some of its funds to Irish educational and charitable purposes, a phrase designed to embrace projects of benefit to the Catholic majority. In this way it was hoped to lessen the bitter hostility to the payment of tithe and take some of the steam out of the demand for Repeal. The extreme right wing of the Whig party, led by Stanley, but supported by Grey, regarded any measure to divert some part of the Church's revenue in this way as an attack on the Protestant religion and opposed it strenuously. They were ready to introduce legislation to remove the worst abuses in the collection of the tithe, which was done, but they attacked the so-called 'appropriation clauses' with such vigour that the proposal to divert some of the Anglican revenues was dropped. Moreover Stanley succeeded in 1833 in getting a Coercion Act giving special powers to the executive to deal with the violence that arose from evictions, excessive rents and tithe, leaving O'Connell and the Irish members in the House unsatisfied and bitter.

The crisis came next year when Stanley demanded the renewal of the Coercion Act, then about to expire. Once again the Cabinet was divided between the more liberal element, anxious to go some way towards modifying the exclusive position of the Protestant Church and if possible coming to a working arrangement with O'Connell, and the diehard Protestants who saw in every such move a threat to their religion. It was a ding-dong battle in the course of which fiery little Lord John declared his intention of raising the question of appropriations and of insisting on the appointment of a commission to enquire into Church revenues in Ireland. Stanley, Graham Richmond and Ripon all then resigned. According to Punch 'Jonney had upset the Coach.' Meanwhile the content of the new coercion bill had still to be settled, the key point at issue being whether the prohibition against the holding of public meetings, which it was feared might incite people to violence, should be continued. Over this there was some very pretty manoeuvring instigated by that stormy petrel the Chancellor, Lord Brougham, who apparently gave O'Connell the impression that the prohibition would be dropped and, when this was not done, the latter accused Lord Althorp, that most honest of politicians, of double dealing and of having been behind the misleading conversations. Lord Althorp promptly resigned and Lord Grey, weary of the wrangling and the burden of office, equally promptly seized the opportunity of resigning himself.

This placed William IV in a difficult position. Though he had cooperated with the Whigs over the Reform Bill the King was at heart a Tory, but there seemed little chance that either

Wellington or Peel could command a majority in the Commons at this stage, though the Tories were still in a majority in the Lords, a circumstance that did not make the position of the Whig government an easy one. For most of the leading Whigs William IV had little personal liking. Indeed he had a strong aversion to two of them, Lord John Russell, whom he designated as 'that young man' in a tone which it is not difficult to imagine, and Lord Brougham whose radical views and eccentric behaviour he heartily disliked and distrusted. If possible he would therefore have preferred a coalition and when he sent for Melbourne it was with this in mind. It was a task which, very respectfully, Melbourne declined. On 10 July, in reply to the royal invitation, he wrote a tactful letter pointing out that the views held by prospective colleagues on the thorny question of the Irish Church were so diverse that he did not think he would be able to form a ministry acceptable to the King. Meanwhile in a private audience Althorp told William IV that the clauses in the Coercion Bill would have to be dropped. Unless Althorp could be persuaded to withdraw his resignation Melbourne would certainly have refused to accept the headship of the ministry, in spite of Lord John beseeching him to save the country from the alternative, which was a Tory government, because since he was in the Lords himself it was essential that he should be able to rely on Althorp to manage the Commons. If however the latter, on the basis of dropping the clauses against public meetings in Ireland, to which he had always been opposed, could be persuaded to join the ministry, then Melbourne was prepared to form and head a government. His oft repeated remark that it was all 'a damn bore' was half truth, half affectation. Underneath his flippancy and nonchalance Melbourne was not a man to shirk doing his duty and had he not taken the Treasury it is difficult to know to whom the King could have turned.

Melbourne's position was not an enviable one. The Whigs were not a united party committed to a well-defined policy, and in addition their majority in the Commons was not sufficiently large to make the Irish vote of no consequence. Throughout his term of office the problem of Ireland was to remain a constant complication. Conscious of the weakness of his position Melbourne placed his brother-in-law, Lord Duncannon at the Home Office, feeling it essential that whoever held that key office should be somebody on whom he could rely. Moreover O'Connell got on well with Duncannon, and this, if not vital, was highly desirable. Much as he might wish to do so it was not always possible for him to pick colleagues who would be acceptable to the King. Lord Brougham remained Lord Chancellor and proved a difficult member of the Cabinet, of which he clearly regarded himself as a leading member, giving it out that he thought it better that 'Lamb should be at the Treasury' thereby casting himself for the role of king-maker. Brougham was always a highly controversial figure; the light in which he is regarded depends very much on the political angle from which he is viewed. His enemies, and they were many, considered him an egotistical 'show off' always seeking the limelight, his friends a convinced radical who made substantial contributions to popular education. Certainly in the new ministry he was determined to make his presence felt. It was highly characteristic of him that he should attend a select committee of the House of Commons inquiring into the vexed question of taxes on newspapers, wearing his robes and cocked hat, so that in his presence the members had to rise and uncover. Melbourne's personal feelings towards him were ambivalent, swinging from active dislike to a wry affection. He told Victoria, who with her usual forthrightness judged him a bad man, that he had heart and feeling, but was too susceptible and acted on impulse. *The Times,* whose editor disliked him, wrote on 25 July, shortly after the formation of the new ministry, 'Lord Melbourne would soon find him out, as the honest men of the community were an over match for knaves', while on 19 August he declared that the Chancellor acted under the influence of a morbid excitement 'seldom evinced by those of His Majesty's subjects who are suffered to remain masters of their own actions,' and a contemporary cartoon portrayed Brougham and the Prime Minister as 'the Wolf and the Lamb.'

Lord John Russell was difficult in a different way. He could be described as a politician in blinkers in that he was obsessed by his own convictions and correspondingly difficult to manipulate. He was also given to sudden impulsive utterances that could place the ministry as a whole in an awkward position when some speech of his indicated too decided an approach to an issue that Melbourne was anxious to surround with an aura of vague possibilities; moreover the King's dislike of him was an added inconvenience. Nor did the King like Sir John Hobhouse, Byron's old friend, who now went to the Ministry of Woods and Forests. Palmerston at the Foreign Office was a mixed blessing. He was inclined to ride roughshod over the susceptibilities of foreign powers, had an itch to interfere in their internal affairs, and was prone to read them lectures over their handling of them. Melbourne personally showed little interest in foreign affairs. He was fundamentally English in his outlook, had spent little time even in Paris, which he had visited with Lady Caroline, and confessed to a dislike of holding conversations in French. Moreover, though prepared to defend British interests when he thought that necessary, he was averse to looking for trouble or interfering. He had long been aware of Palmerston's disposition, which he conceded was based on the English love of liberty, to interfere in the affairs of other countries, a disposition which he admitted to be praiseworthy, but was not therefore the less dangerous, the less embarrassing to this country or the less offensive to foreign powers. If some of his colleagues were difficult he had staunch and dependable allies in the Marquis of Lansdowne, his old friend Lord Holland and the level-headed Lord Althorp, Earl Spencer's eldest son. It would be difficult to find anybody more typically English than this noble lord. Nothing but a sense of duty, of what he owed to his family and rank, kept him in politics. At heart he was a countryman. He was a poor speaker yet a most successful leader of the Commons because of his patent honesty and unwavering loyalty to the things in which he believed. How valuable he would be to the new government the events of the next few months were to show.

Meanwhile the ship of state managed to keep afloat, though by November the diarist Creevy was pitying Melbourne 'raw as he is in the concern and with such a crew'. If he pitied himself he did not show it, continuing apparently imperturbable in public and engaging in his usual social activities. Emily Eden commented on the fact, writing 'I suppose things are going well for I never saw people in greater glee than the ministers are. Lord Melbourne is in the highest state of spirits which seems to me odd for the Prime Minister of the Country.' The occasion that caused this remark was a very cheerful dinner-party but the remainder of the night, 16 October, was less cheerful. Leaving the table Melbourne and his friends returned to Westminster only to find the Commons ablaze. It was perhaps symbolic that Melbourne should see the shrine of so much tradition that he valued go up in flames before him. For some hours he stayed watching the conflagration and encouraging the men who were attempting to control the blaze. Emily Eden, whose brother Lord Auckland was a member of the ministry, was someone to whom over the past two years Lord Melbourne had become warmly attached. His sister Emily, when she had first brought them together at her house, Panshanger, in 1832, had hoped that the meeting might have led to marriage. Emily was a complete contrast to Lady Caroline. Where Caroline was romantic she was cool, almost astringent, responsible and well adjusted in her half-amused acceptance of life. Like Caroline, and so many intelligent women of her day, she too was a novelist and it would be difficult to find a greater contrast than between 'Glenarvon' and 'The Semi-Attached Couple' so Austenish in its observation of contemporary society. When Melbourne first met Miss Eden she was thirty-five, by the standards of the times a confirmed spinster and by her own a happy one. Melbourne, according to her own account, showed her the greatest attention but she wrote, rather smugly, that 'by the blessing of Providence I do not take to him at all'. In any case she considered herself too old for marriage, but even had her thoughts so inclined she found him less agreeable than his brother Frederick, whom she had met before, while considering him probably just as wicked. Moreover she found it, as did so many people, difficult to size him up or to know quite how to take his outrageous and paradoxical remarks. Also she thought he swore too much, 'damn' being too often on his lips. Certainly at times his conversation could be described as 'robust' and Creevy reports on his lack of delicacy. Yet even by the end of her visit to Panshanger Emily was beginning to revise her opinion under the softening influence of his intelligence and charm and soon they became good friends. By the time that he became Prime Minister they were seeing a good deal of one another, though, as she was at pains to point out, without having any 'sinister design'.

New worries, when he was glad of her sympathy and even partisanship, were not far off. Lord Althorp had only reluctantly resumed his old role as Leader of the House of Commons and when his father died on 10 November the opportunity of an honourable escape arrived with his translation to the Upper House. Somehow Melbourne had to find a man to replace Althorp as Chancellor of the Exchequer, which perhaps did not present too many difficulties as Althorp was hardly a financial genius, and as Leader of the Commons. To find some-one acceptable both to the Commons and to the King was a much greater problem. In accordance with the correct procedure Melbourne wrote to William IV, who at that time was at Brighton, asking whether the latter wished him to make fresh arrangements to fill the vacancy or if he had any other arrangements in mind and requesting leave to wait on the King at Brighton to discuss the new situation. This letter can be, and has been, interpreted differently. It could have been couched in these terms merely as a formal mark of the respect which a man of Melbourne's background and training would automatically show to the King, a keeping up the pretence, becoming increasingly hollow in practice, that the choice of minsters still remained with the King, or it could have been a discreet hint suggesting a change of minsters by a man discouraged by the difficulties of his situation. Emily Eden, who probably was in as good a position as anyone to know the truth, said that Melbourne had gone to Brighton to propose a new Chancellor of the Exchequer without foreseeing any difficulty and that his colleagues, who were dining with her and her brother that day, far from expecting any crisis, thought that the Prime Minister would be back in London that evening because there was so little to discuss. Nevertheless there had been some indications that should have warned him of possible complications. When the King had first asked Melbourne to form a government in July he had inquired anxiously whether he could feel secure against the new government introducing legislation of which he could not approve. In reply Melbourne, while reassuring the King about the present, was careful to reserve future freedom of action, saying that the ecclesiastical establishments of both England and Ireland needed remodelling and that as Prime Minister he must feel free to offer advice on any measures that might become necessary. Basically the King was a Tory and though personally civil enough to Melbourne the latter knew that he would have preferred Wellington and Peel to any Whig ministers. Moreover in replying to Melbourne's request for leave to come to Brighton the King made the somewhat significant remark that the present government was 'mainly founded upon the personal weight and influence possessed by Earl Spencer in the House of Commons' and that the control of that House was vital to the administration because it was in a minority in the Lords. Melbourne therefore had some grounds for suspecting the royal intentions.

On the Prime Minister's arrival at Brighton he soon found that William IV found reasons for objecting to all the suggestions he put forward, and particularly to the proposal that Lord John should be entrusted with the Leadership of the House. Finally the King asked Melbourne to stay over-night in order that he might have more time to consider these proposals. Next morning before he left for London he received a letter from William IV the gist of which was that he, the King, 'did not think it would be acting fairly or honourably by his lordship to call on the Viscount for the continuation of his services in a position of which the tenure appeared to the King to be so precarious.' In other words William IV dismissed his Prime Minister while he still had a majority in the Commons, and by intimating his intention to send for Wellington and Peel had produced a first-class constitutional crisis. Much that George III could have done at the beginning of his reign with perfect constitutional propriety would be looked at askance if done by William IV, while what he could do would in turn be regarded as a serious breach of accepted convention if done by Victoria. Even within Melbourne's life the relation between the King and his ministers was revolutionised. When George III became King in 1760 though it was recognised that the King could not choose his chief minister in the face of the disapproval of the Commons, he had means of influencing that House which were not available to the Crown to anything like the same extent after the passing of the Reform Act. Moreover in the eighteenth century it was still the accepted convention that members ought to support the King's ministers unless they could show with some appearance of credibility that they were acting against the national interest. During the Regency, and later throughout the reigns of George IV amd William IV, a combination of their respective characters and ability with the changes that were taking place in British society, had reduced the royal choice to largely a negative one. The sovereign could still make considerable difficulties over accepting either a policy or a minister of which he did not approve, but if opposed to the will of the majority in the Commons he discovered that his hand could be forced, as had been that of William IV over the proposal to create peers should this prove necessary to pass the Reform Bill. Nevertheless the change had been veiled by a respectful tact, apparent consultation and persuasion in such a way that the situation had left the King with an illusion of power. Melbourne, relying on the Whig majority in the Commons, even though the clash between the oldaristocratic core and the radicals and the need to conciliate the Irish vote did produce some internal party weakness, may be excused for not having expected more than obstruction from the King. According to Emily Eden his dismissal was as great a surprise to him as it was to his colleagues because in his conversations with William IV he had never considered that such difficulties as there were in reconstructing the administration were serious and had never emphasised clashes in the Cabinet as a reason for not continuing the administration. Emily judged him ill used.

Melbourne's personal reaction was a mixed one; as usual he could see both sides. As soon as he received the royal communication he dashed off a letter to Lord Holland giving him the news and writing with his customary moderation 'I am not surprised at his decision' nor, he continued, in view of the royal dislike of Russell and Brougham and his apprehension of the measures they were likely to recommend against the Church, 'do I know that I can actually condemn it.' Melbourne himself was almost immediately to be given an example of Brougham's irresponsibilty which made him in future almost as unwilling to see the Chancellor in high office as was the King. On Brougham coming to see Melbourne late that night on his return the ex-Prime Minister told him in confidence what had happened, on the strict understanding that the news should not be made public until the rest of his colleagues had been informed. Brougham, however, could not resist the temptation to leak the surprising news to *The Times* so that next morning ministers received their first intimation of their dismissal from that journal. Melbourne personally made no further comment on the King's action, though his remark to Emily that he did not like to tell his story and that he hated to be thought ill used would seem to indicate that he felt his dismissal more than his pride would allow him to admit and that it certainly was not something for which he had been in any way responsible. Later he told Victoria that it had been a very disagreeable affair, and subsequent to his dismissal he told Lord Holland that he had no doubt that his government would have continued to enjoy the confidence of the Commons. Nevertheless, whatever his private feelings, he acquiesced in the royal action with a calm that infuriated his more belligerent colleagues and gave some colour to the supposition that in some way he must have been part author of his own dismissal. Indeed to people with a more positive, aggressive attitude towards life Melbourne, with his belief that when in doubt it was better to do nothing, combined with his propensity to indulge in mocking comments more often apt to mystify than enlighten his listeners as to his genuine feelings, must have been a singularly baffling man with whom to have dealings. At times he can be equally baffling to his biographers, for whom it is always a temptation to suppose that their subject was consistent in his moods and avowals. To have been annoyed at the way one has been treated, to have done nothing consciously to create a particular situation, and yet privately to be glad that one's hand has been forced probably summed up Melbourne's feelings. At least he was free of all the worries and responsibilities of running the country and coping with difficult colleagues.

Sir Robert Peel, for long Wellington's right-hand man, and at his wish premier designate, was apparently as surprised as Melbourne if not more so, at the turn of events. In November Peel had been on holiday in Italy, from where he had to be fetched post haste, no simple task when travellers and couriers depended on sailing ships and horses for transport. Until Peel could get back Wellington substituted as deputy Prime Minister, though he now felt too old to fill that office permanently. The summons brought no great pleasure to Sir Robert, who, though he certainly considered it his duty to assume office at the royal command, was too astute a politician to believe that the reaction against the reforming policy of the Whigs was sufficiently strong to give him the necessary majority in the Commons. On the Lords, under the control of Wellington, he knew he could rely. In any case he could not go on with the present House of Commons, and a general election took place in December. The results were sufficient to show that the political tide was turning; the Tories won about a hundred seats, but they remained in the minority as against a combination of the Irish, the Radicals and the authentic Whigs. Peel therefore found himself the leader of a minority government, while Melbourne was placed in the embarrassing position of being uncomfortably dependent on allies that he did not trust. The Whigs had never been a united party and now the radical wing and those on its fringes pressed him to rally round him all men of progressive views. This was a course of action far from his inclinations. Personally he still accepted the traditional view that the Crown had a right to expect that its chosen ministers should be given a reasonable chance to put their policies before the House. Moreover on questions of further reforms Peel's attitude was much nearer to Melbourne's own than that of his late colleague Lord John. Peel had made this clear on the eve of the general election by issuing to his constituents the so-called Tamworth Manifesto in which he declared that he now accepted the Reform Act and that far from attempting to put the clock back he was prepared for a programme of moderate reform. On this his personal record had been good. As Home Secretary under Liverpool he had carried through such important measures as the formation of the metropolitan police and the abolition of the death penalty for about a hundred felonies; and his concern about the need for improving the working conditions for children in factories was a good deal more enlightened than Melbourne's, who thought that the children were not overworked and that it was wrong to prevent parents from sending their children to work there at whatever age they pleased. Had it not been for the accident of birth and background Melbourne might well have been happier as a colleague of Peel – not that the two men were personally congenial – than as the leader of a party which was either genuinely pressing for reforms, as the Radicals were, or who at least believed that it ought to be associated with them. It was not only his more progressive colleagues who were harrying him to take some action. The Irish were prepared to support him but they wanted their price. One of the effects of the election had been to re-create the uneasy understanding between O'Connell and the Whigs. Dissatisfied as he was with the fruits of his previous co-operation with them O'Connell knew that

Melbourne was at least vaguely sympathetic to the Irish grievances where these concerned the Church, though he remained adamant on the need to preserve law and order in that violence-rent country, and that Lord John was committed to the cause of appropriating some of the revenues of the Anglican Church to serve the whole community, while from the Tories nothing in this way could be expected. The more aggressive Whigs, when the new Parliament met, were anxious to join battle with the Tories over the choice of a new Speaker in the Commons, hoping to replace Sutton Manners by Abercromby, and for this they needed Irish support. For this purpose a meeting was held with O'Connell in February 1835 at Lichfield House. Melbourne, who disliked the idea of co-operation, did not mean this to be more than a temporary expedient, but though nothing was specifically arranged with regard to future consultations, after their success in the election of Abercromby as Speaker by 316 to 306 the logic of events condemned him to rely on a *de facto* alliance. At the end of six weeks, after a series of minor defeats, the combination of Lord John and the Irish party proved too strong for Peel. He was defeated on the former's motion to appropriate part of the revenues of the Established Church in Ireland and, convinced that it was impossible to carry on, he resigned. For the King, as Melbourne told Victoria, it was a bitter pill to swallow. He had now no alternative to asking Melbourne to form a new government.

Though in some ways Melbourne came back with a position weakened by an eroded majority in the Commons, in other respects the break-up of his first administration eased his personal difficulties. For the first time he was free, in a way that he had not been when he had taken over from Lord Grey, to choose his own colleagues. This to him was of the first importance. He was still sufficiently a man of the eighteenth century to believe that who did things was more important than what they planned to do. He wrote 'difficulties with respect to the government of the country, with respect to further measures, seem to me to be little or nothing'. Here his aim was merely to keep things ticking over quietly. With regard to colleagues he was less complaisant. His early months in office had convinced him that some of these men would create trouble for any Prime Minister who included them in his administration. Here he intended to be tough. As far as it lay politically in his power he was determined to exclude any man likely to upset his colleagues or act in such a way as to embarrass the government and then leave him, Melbourne, to deal with the consequences. Also it would be an advantage to exclude anyone who, because of his policies or his personality, was likely to upset the King. Though as a matter of principle he treated the monarch with all possible deference and respect he was not unaware of the fact that it would be he, as Prime Minister, who would suffer most from the backlash of the royal dislike. Nevertheless he was realist enough to know that a Cabinet so composed was only a pipe dream; some difficult colleagues he would have to accept.

Lord John Russell could at times be difficult. Unlike Melbourne he was more inclined to see issues in black and white; sometimes he acted on impulse, committing the government in ways that to Melbourne seemed quite unnecessary; moreover William IV disliked him, muttering that he never knew what he meant. Nevertheless he and Melbourne got on well together. They agreed on the policy to be followed in Ireland on Church matters, and on the need for municipal reform both in that country and in England. As he told the King after a misunderstanding, though Lord John might act 'through indiscretion and misconception' he was 'utterly incapable of anything of an underhand or clandestine character'. Moreover he was essential to the stability of the ministry as the best Leader of the House. Melbourne accordingly placed him at the Home Office and took tolerantly his decision to reverse his own policy towards the Dorchester labourers by repatriating them. Melbourne never had any intention of excluding little Lord John but he would like to have done so in the case of Lord Palmerston whom he feared might upset foreign rulers with his tactless advocacy of liberal views and his propensity to take a blustering line, thus entangling the government in what to Melbourne were quite unnecessary complications. But Palmerston was adamant; it was the Foreign Office or nothing and he was too important to be left out. Also, though one can only guess how far Melbourne was influenced by such considerations, Palmerston had a firm ally in Lady Cowper, his beloved sister Emily. Rumour indeed said that they were lovers, and certainly the new Foreign Secretary, though a bachelor, had the kind of reputation that had led *The Times*, whose editor did not like him, to allude to him in its columns as 'Lord Cupid'. But Melbourne did contrive to keep out the most radical troublemakers. Chief of these was Lord Brougham. He was so unpredictable in his sponsorship of radical ideas, and so extravagant in his support of them, and in general had been so self-opinionated a colleague in the previous administration, that Melbourne was determined not to allow him to become Lord Chancellor a second time. With his usual tact and kindness he tried to soften the blow by telling Brougham that the Chancellorship was to be put into commission for the time being, implying that Brougham's theatrical progress which he had lately made through Scotland had so annoyed the King that some such measure had become temporarily necessary. There was some truth in this excuse. William IV disliked the ex-chancellor intensely and Melbourne felt that 'even if all the rest agreed to let Brougham in, I could not bring myself to force him on the King.' The Great Seal remained in commission until January 1836.

By that time Melbourne felt himself to be more firmly in the saddle and to Brougham's fury appointed Lord Cottenham. He had long come to the decision that 'if left out he would indeed be dangerous, but if taken in he would simply be destructive. We may have little chance to go on without him, but to go on with him would be impossible.' When a friend asked him how he got on with the new Chancellor he made the characteristic reply 'Oh! capitally; I am like a man who had broken with his termagant mistress, and married the best of cooks.' Another potential candidate for office whose views were too radical for Melbourne's taste was Lord Durham, whose offensive behaviour to Lord Grey in Cabinet meetings over the Reform Bill had made Melbourne long to knock him down. Later, after the Canadian episode, when for once he had entrusted Durham with responsibility, Haydon the painter, to whom Melbourne sat for one of his many portraits, making conversation during the sitting 'spoke of Lord Durham's return – Dead silence'. Temporarily he shelved the problem of what should be done about Durham by sending him back to Russia, where since 1832 he had been ambassador-extraordinary at the Czar's court. Meanwhile, having disposed of the two most likely trouble-makers the new Prime Minister felt that he could look forward with reasonable confidence to a harmonious Cabinet. His brother-in-law Lord Ducannon was now Privy Seal; another political friend Spring Rice, with whom he used to correspond over Ireland, was promoted to be Chancellor of the Exchequer; while Lord Lansdowne presided over the Council and Lord Holland returned to his old office as Chancellor of the Duchy of Lancaster. Lord Auckland, Emily Eden's brother, returned to the Admiralty until in September he was sent to India as Governor General. This latter appointment had personal consequences for Melbourne as, to his very genuine sadness, Emily went with him. As a result of this careful selection of future colleagues Melbourne viewed his second term of office with something like tranquillity. Even William IV seemed resigned to having him back; at one time he had told Peel that he could never give his confidence to Whig ministers but when Melbourne, in the process of resuming office, asked if he could depend on receiving it he received the brusque reply 'Good God! I would not have sent for you if I didn't mean to do so.' He did not like Whigs but possibly he disliked Melbourne, who was used to Royalty and knew how to treat them, as little as he disliked any of them. Melbourne once told Victoria that the King was always very civil to him personally.

Even in Ireland the arrangements he made seemed reasonably satisfactory. O'Connell was still a problem. His support in the Commons was more necessary than ever yet Melbourne felt that he dare not gratify his legal ambitions, ambitions which his reputation at the Irish Bar fully justified. This was partly because English politicians, mostly drawn as they were from the gentry, had a contempt for him, disliking both his policy and his over-dramatic speeches full of personal abuse, but also because Melbourne personally suspected him of entertaining far more subversive plans than he probably contemplated. Lady Morgan, Lady Caroline's confidante, herself both Irish and a novelist of some reputation, once described her fellow countrymen as 'this susceptible but injudicious nation . . . more willing to submit to injuries than insults' and the problem of finding the right people to put in charge of its affairs was not easy. Lord John as Home Secretary, together with Melbourne and the rest of the Cabinet were responsible for policy but it was important to choose a Lord Lieutenant and Chief Secretary on whose co-operation they could rely. Accordingly it was decided to appoint Lord Mulgrave, who got on well with Lord John, as

Lord Lieutenant and Lord Morpeth as Chief Secretary. They were satisfactory but not outstanding appointments. The man who was to do more during the next five years to smooth the government's path in Ireland was Thomas Drummond whom Melbourne chose as Under-Secretary. It was an imaginative choice. For thirteen years Drummond had been in the Irish Ordnance Survey Department. He knew the country at first hand and could appreciate its problems in a way that no politician fresh from Westminster could ever hope to do. It was to his on-the-spot handling of difficult situations, to his even-handed administration, which was very much in line with Melbourne's own policy that Roman Catholics should be given a full share in the favours of government, that much of the comparative calm which prevailed until his death in 1840 must be attributed. It was a challenging assignment summed up by a London ballad singer as

> Och, Dublin city there's no doubting
> Bates every city upon the say,
> There you'll hear O'Connell spouting,
> And Lady Morgan making tay;
> For this the capital of the finest nation
> With charming pisantry on a frightful sod
> Fighting like divils for conciliation
> An' hating each other for the love of God.

and Melbourne should be given some credit for choosing so competent a team.

7

THE MINISTRY OF
COMPROMISE

MELBOURNE'S position on resuming office was not enviable. He was too astute not to realise the difficulties that lay ahead even though he was thinking in terms of Westminster politics rather than taking a wider view of the needs of the country where railways were revolutionising transport and communications and where the rapid process of urbanisation was creating appalling problems of sanitation and health. Such matters, according to his creed, were not the responsibility of government; what concerned him was the weakness of the ministry in Parliament where the result of the last election had reflected the growing national support for the Tories. For Tories he had no dislike as such. When trying to break down some of Victoria's prejudices against them he implied that they were neither better nor worse than other politicians. Indeed he had more in common with the more moderate Tories than he had with the extreme Radicals, and if he could have secured their support in 1836 he would have been only too glad to preside over a mixed ministry, particularly as in 1835 Stanley and Graham, who represented the right wing in Grey's government, crossed the floor of the House and threw in their lot with them. For the next six years Melbourne had to run the country with the knowledge that his political enemies had a majority in the House of Lords while in the Commons, faced with a formidable and intelligent body of Tories led by Peel and now reinforced by Stanley and Graham, he was increasingly dependent for his majority on two groups, the Irish and the Radicals, both of which had to be handled with extreme care if they were to be persuaded to give effective support to the Whig administration. It is this situation which explains much of the apparent barrenness of Melbourne's second administration. The House of Lords was still immensely strong. It is true it had lost its control over money bills but before the Parliament Act of 1912 it could reject other bills out of hand and there was nothing that the Commons could do about it short of refusing supply. This was a step no government ever dared to take. Even when the Lords did not reject bills outright they could cut them to pieces with wrecking amendments that totally altered their character and made them incapable of achieving the purpose for which they had been designed. Although in the crisis of the Reform Bill public opinion had been so solidly behind the Whigs that the Upper House had been forced to give way without the creation of new peers, none of the legislation that Melbourne's ministry tried to bring forward had this national appeal. Indeed possibly more people agreed with the Lords over such issues as Ireland, or even radical reforms at home, than did with Melbourne and his ministers. One solution would have been to create more Whig peers and Lord John would have liked this to have been done gradually over a period of years in order to strengthen the party in the Lords. This was an expedient Melbourne was unwilling to adopt, even when Victoria's coronation would have given him an excellent opportunity to do so. In the same way he turned down Lord John's more revolutionary suggestion for the creation of life peers. Fundamentally Melbourne's allegiance was to his own order and he preferred to struggle on with the Lords as a perpetual menace to the success of his legislative programme.

The attitude of the Lords seems to have worried him less than the difficulties created by his colleagues. He enjoyed the debates in the House; there was some fun there, he said, and he bore philosophically the attacks on him, against which on occasion he was capable of defending himself stoutly. What vexed and wore him down was the constant bickering among his nominal supporters. To some extent these were due to personal strains and clashes of temperament. Lord John lacked tact. He seemed to care very little for other people's opinions or when he trod on their toes. Proud, shy and sensitive, he held himself aloof from the people he was supposed to be leading, animated by a conviction that Russells had a right to command and other lesser mortals the duty to obey. Occasionally also by giving voice to his own personal views in an 'off-the-cuff' speech he plunged the ministry into embarrassments from which it took Melbourne time and energy to extract it. Inevitably he was the butt of many political squibs. Bulwer Lytton lampooned him:

> How formed to lead if not too proud to please,
> His frame would fire you but his manners freeze.

These were hardly qualities for a successful Leader of the House. A Whig of the old school, his radicalism took the form of securing civil liberties which would round out the Reform Act but not get beyond it, though later he was to adopt more radical views on constitutional issues. Such limited objectives did not content the more extreme radicals of 1835 and '36 who were pressing for shorter Parliaments, a wider franchise and the use of the ballot in parliamentary elections; it was they who christened him 'Finality Jack'. Lord Howick, Lord Grey's eldest son, was another touchy, difficult person, very tender of his father's reputation as a reformer and not lacking in a belief in his own right and capacity to hold similar high office. Lord Glenelg at the Colonial Office, once difficulties blew up over Canada in 1837, was another member of the Cabinet who proved more of a liability than an asset. Tensions within the Cabinet were also a reflection of the lack of harmony between the main body of the Whigs and their radical and Irish supporters, who by no means necessarily wanted to follow the same policies, so that Melbourne found himself doing a balancing act between the two, now attempting to placate O'Connell and his friends, now trying to mollify the Radicals and their Dissenting allies.

Of the two the Radicals were perhaps the easier to satisfy. In the first place they realised that lukewarm though Melbourne was the Tories were likely to be even more hostile, and, possibly even more important, much of what they wanted had solid middle-class support behind it, which made their programme politically more attractive to the government. The result was three major pieces of legislation spread over the six years of Melbourne's administration. The first of these was concerned with the reform of the municipal corporations which were still very much bastions of local privilege; many of them were corrupt, many of them self-perpetuating oligarchical, and in 1833 the Whigs had appointed a commission to report on their condition and powers. The Whigs had a political interest in their reshaping. In the past they had exercised considerable power over the election of MPs and, though diminished, this had not disappeared with the Reform Act. Many corporations continued to be Tory strongholds and the Whigs as politicians, as well as the Radicals as reformers, were anxious to remove this threat before the next election, when the Tory vote might be expected to be still greater. This was a bill which the Tories dare not oppose in principle, though the Lords contrived to introduce into the newly formed elected councils a more oligarchical element in the shape of aldermen. They would also have liked a property qualification for councillors. On this occasion Melbourne and Brougham were in agreement and fought stoutly side by side, while in the Cabinet the Prime Minister threw his authority on the side of a household franchise, based on the payment of rates, rather than restricting it, as in the case of the parliamentary franchise, to those tenements of a minimum value of £10. Though he had little liking for democracy and popular control he was always aware of the danger of giving too little, too late. The result of the Municipal Corporations Act was to create the framework for democratic urban self-government under a mayor and elected council.

An equally important but less publicised reform was carried through in 1836. Before this date there had been no machinery for the official registration of births, marriages and deaths, regarded as the responsibility of the Church, which maintained parish registers for this purpose. A strong section of the Radicals were Dissenters who resented this overall authority of the Anglican Church; they resented the payment of church rates and the fact that legal marriages could only be solemnised by the official clergy. Partly to placate them, but also to meet the needs of a new statistically hungry society, it was decided to appoint a Registrar General and to use the local divisions of 'unions', set up under the new Poor Law Amendment Act of

1834 for the provision of workhouses and Poor Law administration, as registration districts. For the first time in British history it was possible to know the exact age of a growing population and to have a basis for vital statistics, so necessary in a world of growing technology. No longer was it necessary for factory inspectors, struggling to enforce the provisions of the act that prohibited the employment of children under the age of nine in cotton mills, to look at their teeth as if they were estimating the age of horses. Of more immediate importance to the Dissenters was the fact that they could now be married in their own chapels, though the Lords did insert a clause by which the registrar must be present at the ceremony to make it legal. Church rates, however, proved too thorny a subject to handle in any way that would both satisfy the Dissenters and not antagonise the Church, and the attempt to deal with this had to be dropped. Melbourne, while agreeing to the proposal, told Lord John that he thought the Church would defeat it and he proved right. His views on Dissenters varied; in the mass he disliked the narrowness of their views but, as he once told Victoria, there was something to be said for them as servants in that they did not drink and were not always wanting time off to go to race-meetings. The other major sop given to the Radicals was the introduction of the penny post, associated with the name of Rowland Hill, though it must be remembered that a penny was still a considerable sum to a poor person when a labourer might only earn twelve shillings a week and some considerably less in bad times. But to the world of industry and to the middle class it was a boon and one that struck at the aristocratic privileges of 'franking letters', that is sending them for nothing. Victoria was sufficiently interested to ask Melbourne to get her a franked letter which she could keep as a memento of the past.

But though Melbourne went some way to satisfy the Radicals by these measures he was determined to divert them from any direct attack on the Church. Personally, though he was interested in theology, so that Victoria commended his clear exposition of the contents of religious authors and sermons, he was not a churchman except by birth and breeding. Indeed the Queen commented archly on the fact that he avoided being at Windsor on a Sunday, pleading either that he could not get away or that he was unwell. But he realised that to tamper with the Church was political dynamite. By the thirties it was under attack from three sides. The established Church had no appeal for the intelligent working class, who regarded it with indifference before the struggle of the Reform Bill and with hostility after it on account of the way in which the majority of bishops had voted in critical divisions in the House of Lords. The Dissenters, whether artisans or middle-class voters, had genuine grievances that arose out of the Church's privileged position. Not all of these were connected with tithes and church rates; for instance only a member of the Established Church could take a degree at Oxford or Cambridge, or be accepted as a fellow of the College of Physicians. Even more fundamental and dangerous were the attacks that came from within. Many earnest Anglicans, particularly those of an Evangelical turn of mind, were seriously worried by the state of the contemporary Church, where some bishops were almost clerical princes enjoying huge revenues while others could hardly sustain the most modest expenses incurred by their office; where some livings were rich and others could hardly provide for the proverbial church-mouse; where pluralities abounded and where the presentation to livings so often lay in either private, college or government hands, thus providing patronage that was habitually used to gain political support. It is easy to overpaint the picture of a venal and corrupt Church. Such a picture would be unjust to the many earnest clergy who held sees and benefices, but it was a picture which its enemies, by selecting their evidence, could present without straying beyond what many people knew to be true. The mass of the Tories however would rally, as they had rallied since the reign of Queen Anne, to the call of 'the Church in danger'. Too many of its attackers came from the ranks of Melbourne's supporters for him to be able to ignore their demands for ecclesiastical reform but political prudence dictated that these should be carried out without arousing too much Tory fury. To achieve this the Church must be manoeuvred into putting its own house in order, so that the need for reform from outside should no longer seem so blatant. A committee of inquiry was already in existence, and during the early months of his second term of office Melbourne himself, Lord John, whom he constantly consulted on Church matters, Lords Cottenham, Lansdowne and Spring Rice, attended its meetings, though gradually more

113

and more was left to Bishop Bloomfield. By the end of the 1836 session the commission had reported and three bills, which could be described as being based on the recommendations of churchmen not politicians, were brought forward to equalise the revenues of the episcopalian sees with the exception of Canterbury, York, Durham and London, and to deal with the evils of pluralities. Perhaps even more important it was decided to make the ecclesiastical commissioners permanent and so take away from the politicians the appearance of interfering directly in the administration of the Church. This did not mean that Melbourne felt that he could now ignore ecclesiastical affairs; he, and later Victoria when she became Queen, took a great deal of care in the appointment of bishops. He was too acutely aware of the importance of personality not to wish the Church to be in the hands of safe moderate men. He also carried through a characteristic compromise over the lack of opportunities for Dissenters to take degrees in England; realising that he could never force Oxford and Cambridge to open their doors to any but members of the Established Church he concurred in the granting of a charter to a new, non-sectarian University of London, in the creation of which Brougham was keenly interested. The Whig Cabinet also dealt with another and most unpopular privilege of the beneficed clergy, namely their right to collect a tithe, an imposition disliked quite as much by Anglican farmers as by Dissenters, by bringing in a bill for the commutation of the tithe into a rent charge, so that the farmer was no longer driven to exasperated fury by having to delay the garnering of the harvest until the rector had collected his tenth sheaf, or of seeing his tenth piglet carried squalling away.

It is common form to accuse Melbourne of having no interest in contemporary social and economic problems, and to some extent the accusation is just. It was private members such as Lord Ashley, better known by his later title of Lord Shaftesbury, who championed the factory workers in a campaign for a ten-hour day, and who demanded and got commissioners appointed to inquire into the employment of children in industry and mines. It was Edwin Chadwick and his friends who campaigned ceaselessly for better urban sanitation. Melbourne shrank fastidiously from anything that was crude; life in the raw never appealed to him. He disliked Dickens for this reason. He thought he had a low debasing style and was

repelled as much by 'low life' and workhouse squalor in fiction
as in fact. Oliver Twist was not for him. Essentially he was a
Londoner, even if he never penetrated into the London that
Dickens knew, in spite of his love for Brocket, and even Brocket
he detested in the winter, which made him only a fair weather
countryman. He knew nothing at first hand of the great
sprawling towns of the midlands and the north. It was natural
that he should have no understanding, and therefore no interest
and sympathy with, the problems of the new industrial society
that was gradually swallowing up the England he knew and
loved. New ideas had no appeal to him and he had little patience
with the views of either Lord Brougham or Lord John on the
need for popular education. Indeed while the latter was
struggling to get his act on education through Parliament
Melbourne confessed to Victoria that 'I daren't say it these
times that I'm against it, but I am'. His attitude was the insular
one that though a system of public education might suit the
Germans, in England it was best left to voluntary efforts, while
as for the proposal to establish Normal Schools for the training
of teachers he thought them likely to breed 'the most conceited
set of blockheads ever known'. Indeed he believed that the poor
in the mass were not susceptible to education, quoting Sir
Walter Scott's question 'Why do you bother the poor? Leave
them alone' with approval. This defeatist attitude that education
could do little for any but the leisured classes sprang both from
his acceptance of a social structure that he had always known
and from an innate belief that 'You had better try to do no good
and then you will get into no scrape.' For this latter view he had
some political justification, at least as far as education was in
issue. Victorian England took religion even more seriously.
Noncomformists would rather find the money to educate their
children in their own schools than risk their being contaminated
by having to learn the catechism in Church schools. When an
attempt was made to provide public education paid for by the
local rates the Dissenters and the Anglicans were in such bitter
opposition that the scheme had to be dropped. Politically there
was no easier way to 'get into a scrape' than to stir up the
hornet's nest of religious prejudice. Nevertheless in spite of
Melbourne's personal aloofness from social problems it is not
fair to dismiss his ministry as barren in this respect. The first
beginnings of Church reforms, the founding of London

University, the remodelling of urban local government, the devising of a national system of registration for births, marriages and deaths, the introduction of the penny post, were all very necessary steps in the modernisation of Britain. Melbourne might often be reluctant to embark on such schemes but he was sufficiently a political realist to accept their political necessity, even though, like the Duke of Plazatoro in *The Gondoliers*, he led his regiment from behind. Driven by the need for Radical support he could have done no less; blocked by the House of Lords dominated by the Duke of Wellington he could have achieved no more. As Lord John pointed out, if the ministry did too little it was in danger of losing its friends, if too much of provoking its enemies. In such circumstances only a man so skilful in personal relations and in compromise could have stayed in power for six cliff-hanging years.

Ireland provided a problem even more intractable than the demands of the Radicals. Here Lord John and Melbourne were at least in full agreement that something must be done for that country, though their motives were not necessarily the same. Melbourne's earlier genuine sympathy for Ireland had been overtaken by a feeling of disillusion; he was slowly reaching the conviction that no legislation, however well intentioned, was likely to win over that country to peaceful co-operation. Yet, because of the number of votes O'Connell controlled, he had to be managed and placated. Melbourne continued neither to like nor to trust him and was as convinced as ever that it would be fatal to confer any office of influence on him. But if nothing could be done for him personally at least an effort must be seen to be made to carry out a policy that would go some way to deal with Irish grievances. Something would have to be done about the Protestant Church in Ireland, something would have to be done to deal with the corrupt state of the Irish corporations, and something would have to be done to tackle the poverty of a country still without a Poor Law. Lord John's motives were more straightforward. He was genuinely convinced of the reality of Irish grievances and, as a matter of principle quite as much as of policy, he flung himself into a 'Justice for Ireland' campaign, arguing that Irishmen could not be denied the civil rights enjoyed by Englishmen.

It could hardly be expected that any persons as oblivious of the economic and social problems that beset their own country as were Lord John and Melbourne would grasp the fact that Irish disorder and violence had similar economic and social roots. As a consequence they attributed those evils almost exclusively to Roman Catholic resentment against an alien Protestant Church. Superficially they had some justification in that much of the current disorder seemed to stem from a widespread refusal to pay the hated tithe in spite of the attempts made to improve its collection in the 1832 act. Tithe, which was resented even in Protestant England – a resentment that had led to the Tithe Act of 1836 – could with justice be even more hated when, as in Ireland, it was levied on a Catholic majority for the upkeep of a Church whose adherents were in a perpetual minority. In Ireland therefore the problem was twofold: the method of levying it needed to be made more equitable and less irritating, which meant, as in England, not only commutation into a rent charge, but some means had to be found of returning to the majority of Irishmen money collected in excess of that genuinely needed by the established Protestant Church to minister to its comparatively small flock since, as Lord John clearly saw, there was very little chance of that flock being augmented by conversions. Herein lay the crux of the difficulty. Since Lord Grey's resignation the Whigs had been committed to the appropriation of surplus Irish Church revenues to the social and charitable needs of the whole country. To the Tories and to men like Stanley and Graham, who had left the Whigs on this issue in 1835, such appropriation represented an attack on Church property that must be resisted at all costs. This is the key to the long-drawn-out political battle over the Irish tithe bills. The details varied from bill to bill but because each bill contained some version of an appropriation clause, each bill in turn was rejected by the Lords. In addition their Lordships made it clear that none of the other measures proposed by Melbourne's administration, in particular bills for remodelling the Irish borough charters on more democratic lines similar to the corporation act of 1835, and the introduction of a Poor Law, would be allowed to pass unless the appropriation clauses were dropped from any tithe bill presented to them. The details of the fight belong more to political history than to a life of Lord Melbourne, though the issue at stake illustrated his comparative political impotency when faced by a hostile House of Lords and demonstrates that if much of his policy was ineffective it is arguable that no man could have done more in his situation.

It illustrates also the strains to which he was subjected as he tried to retain Irish support and to persuade his colleagues that only by compromise could anything be achieved. Finally in 1838 he and Russell had to give way; the appropriation clauses were omitted from the latest tithe bill, which the Lords then allowed to become law. This left the tithe as a rent charge, commuted at the high rate of 75 per cent, which in the first place was to be collected by the landlord and paid by him to the Church. To some extent this obscured the connection between the Church and tithe but only, as O'Connell pointed out, by transferring its unpopularity to the landlords, who were already sufficiently hated by the land-starved peasantry. The government had hardly more success with its plans to remodel the corporations. The Tory majority in the Lords threw out bill after bill in their determination that the control of the Irish boroughs should remain largely in Tory hands, and whereas the Whigs wanted as many Irish boroughs to be included in the provisions of such an act as possible, and wanted the right to vote for the new elective councils to extend to all ratepayers, the Lords insisted on both limiting the number of boroughs brought within the act and on a high £10 franchise, which Melbourne had resisted in the English act. In the end the Tories got their way and what they had been forced to concede to Englishmen under the pressure of public opinion they continued to deny to Irishmen in similar circumstances. The third measure, that of introducing a Poor Law into Ireland, was very largely the work of Lord John and, being opposed mainly by Irish members, who thought it not well adapted to conditions in their country, had a smoother passage in 1837. By that time in England the opposition of the mass of working-class opinion against the Poor Law Amendment Act of 1832 was boiling over in inflamatory speeches and near riots. Therefore with a genuine intention of doing something for Ireland neither Russell nor Melbourne had achieved much to ameliorate conditions in that country and nothing but the conviction that the Tories under Peel would be even less friendly to Irish aspirations kept O'Connell loyal to Melbourne's government.

If Melbourne in his public role met with a series of frustrations, being first jockeyed into sponsoring legislation of which he only half approved and then having the humiliation of seeing it mangled or rejected by the Lords, his private life in 1836 was also full of perplexities and embarrassments. In many ways he was a man made up of opposites. He loved his books, the peace of his library, his periods of solitude, but he needed also the stimulation of society. So it was natural for him to seek reelaxation among his friends, and that among them some woman who could both amuse and interest and give him some outlet for his warmly affectionate nature should come to play an important part in his life. Chance, or Fate, dictated that this woman should be Caroline Norton. A grand-daughter of the Lambs' old friend Richard Brinsley Sheridan, she was beautiful in an arresting way. Fanny Kemble described her vividly as 'Splendidly handsome, of a non-English character of beauty, her rather large and heavy head recalling the grandest Grecian and Italian models, to the latter of which her rich colouring and blue-black braids of hair gave her an additional resemblance'. She had other attractions to back up her beauty. She was a witty epigrammatic conversationalist with a 'comically dramatic manner of narrating things' and the trick of singing both 'pathetic and humorous songs admirably'. Though she had no claims to be a musician she was described as having 'a deep contralto voice, precisely the same in which she always spoke, and which, combined with her always lowered eyelids (downy eye-lids with sweeping silken fringes) gave such incomparably comic efffect to her sharp retorts and ludicrous stories'. She was a woman in whose company it was impossible to be bored. She was in every way a most vivid person, combining the Sheridan wit and charm with a keen interest in the world of politics. Fanny Kemble said she looked as if 'she were made of precious stones, diamonds, emeralds, rubies, sapphires', a comment that well conveys her scintillating personality. Just as Melbourne liked female company she was most at her ease with men, knowing both how to minister to their comfort and to flatter them with her admiration. She was very much the kind of woman who could provide for a harassed Prime Minister just the kind of social relaxation that he craved. At her dinner parties at her small but elegantly appointed house in Storey's Gate he could be sure of meeting interesting people, people that perhaps he might not have met so easily at the table presided over by the more conventionally minded Emily Eden, who viewed Mrs Norton's hold over Lord Melbourne with a notable lack of enthusiasm. Sometimes in turn she dined at South Street, and on the one occasion when Fanny Kemble was honoured by an invitation she left a charming pen-picture of Lord Melbourne reclining on a large crimson ottoman 'surrounded by those three enchanting Sheridan sisters'. Stimulating conversation and interesting company were not to be found only at Storey's Gate. At Holland House, for instance, Lady Holland too had a reputation for collecting people round her who were most worth knowing at any given time, but she could not compete with the gay intimacy of Mrs Norton's parties. Moreover Storey's Gate was a convenient haven on Melbourne's way to and from the House, where he could drop in informally, and where he could always be sure of a sympathetic ear and where he could find a woman able to provide comfort when he was low spirited or anxious about Augustus, and conversely an exhilarating zest for life when what he needed was stimulation. By 1836 it had become a regular routine for him to see her, usually alone, for at least some time every day.

They had first met in December 1830, the year after his name had been linked with that of Lady Brandon. Caroline was unhappily married to George Norton, theyounger brother of Lord Grantley. Beautiful and dowerless, her mother had been only too glad to find any husband of respectable standing who would provide for her daughter, and at nineteen Caroline had been married off without much consideration for her prospect of happiness. As Charlotte was to observe to Elizabeth Bennet in 'Pride and Prejudice,' 'however slight the hope of personal happiness marriage must always be a woman's pleasantest preservation from want', a dictum with which Caroline would hardly have agreed before her own disastrous marriage had run itts course. Contemporaries all agreed that George Norton had the essential qualities of the proverbial cad; he was shifty, mean, a scrounger and withal brutal and vindictive. Caroline soon found that if she were to enjoy the kind of life both economically and socially that was necessary for her she would have both to supplement the family income herself and to exert what influence she could to secure some adequately paid post for her husband. In an age that accepted 'jobs' as a normal method of securing an appointment she wrote to the most influential man on whom her family might be said to have some claim through long friendship, Lord Melbourne, the Home

Secretary, in the hope that he would be able to supplement what she could earn by her pen, by finding some suitable employment for her husband. By this time Mrs Norton had established some reputation both as a poetess and as a novelist, that financial refuge for so many talented penurious nineteenth century ladies. In addition Melbourne knew something of her reputation as an attractive woman who gathered round her entertaining and intelligent people. He therefore answered her letter in person. Mrs Norton was not the woman to let so golden an opportunity slip. The full battery of her charms was employed, not only to obtain a post for her husband but to gain the *cachet* of having the Home Secretary as her known friend and admirer. In so doing her motives were only partly prudential. Melbourne was a most attractive man and, as a companion, could give Mrs Norton just the kind of companionship that she most enjoyed. In some ways the two were very complementary to each other. Though Caroline lacked Lady Melbourne's tact, discretion and worldly wisdom, she had something of her robust mind and keen interest in people, in books and in politics; for Melbourne she filled, in a way that the more rational Emily Eden could never do, a gap that had been empty since his mother's death. By 1836 Caroline had become an important part of his life.

Until then George Norton had shown nothing but complaisance at the way in which their friendship had developed, though in many ways his relations with his wife had gone from bad to worse, a fact of which Melbourne was quite aware. It would not be in character to attribute as a reason for Norton's complaisancy gratitude to the Prime Minister for having found him a paid post as a London magistrate. It was more an insurance policy; as a magistrate his conduct had been sufficiently inadequate to have occasioned public comment from his fellow magistrates, much to Melbourne's irritation. Unsatisfactory though Norton was both as a husband and as a magistrate, if the marriage broke down a very awkward, indeed almost impossible, situation would threaten the continuance of this close friendship. Society did not expect even its public men to observe any very stringent moral code; so long as nominally husband and wife lived together the wife was considered respectable, even though society had a pretty good idea of whatever realities lay behind that facade. In 1836 the crisis came. There had been faults on both sides and Caroline had reacted on many occasions to her husband's meanness and even physical violence with a biting tongue augmented by a corresponding display of physical violence of her own. The trouble was not solely due to personal incompatibility. Norton was a Tory, Caroline a Whig, so that politics were a constant cause of friction. So were the in-laws; George Norton's sister and his wife were mutually antipathetic. Nevertheless Caroline, partly from her deep devotion to her children and partly because society left her no option, continued somehow to rub along with the existing situation. The break came from her husband, who seized the children, which legally he was entitled to do, and turned Caroline out of the house. This would have been distressing enough for Melbourne but George Norton went further; probably either in the hope of substantial hush money or, failing that, substantial damages, he brought a case of criminal conversation with his wife against the Prime Minister. Society buzzed with rumours. The fact that Melbourne had already figured in one such case, that of Lady Brandon, even though it had broken down for lack of evidence, was remembered and the Press, particularly the Tory Press, was full of snide comment, which, aimed at the Prime Minister, could do neither him nor his government any good. Caroline herself, desperate at the loss of her children, and facing the social ruin of divorce, wrote frantic letters to Melbourne, whom she dared no longer meet.

For Melbourne it was an embarrassing, painful period. Conscious of the harm that the scandal might do to his party he tendered his resignation to the King, who refused it. Rumours, which Greville picked up and recorded in his diary, were circulating that Melbourne's political enemies were in some way involved in the attempt, and underhand intrigue was something with which neither William IV nor the Duke of Wellington would care to be associated. Apart from his public position Melbourne was desperately sorry for Caroline, of whom he was genuinely fond. But he realised that there was nothing he could do except counsel patience and prudence, both qualities that Mrs Norton conspicuously lacked. It is true that, partly due to Melbourne's hope that the marriage might yet be patched up and also in the hope of regaining her children, she did beg Norton to take her back. This, presumably from a sense of vindictiveness and a hope of gain, he refused to do. The worry and strain combined with the burden of his office made Melbourne ill. He did what he could emotionally to assure Caroline of how deeply he was distressed for her, and practically by retaining the services of the Attorney General to lead the defence when the case came for trial on 23 June. Melbourne could not appear in Court personally – though he sent an affidavit attesting his innocence of the charge – nor could Caroline. Even Norton could not legally go into the witness box and therefore the case had to be fought out by opposing counsel with the aid of witnesses. When these came to be examined the evidence of any misconduct was suspect and flimsy and Campbell, in a brilliant speech for the defence, had no difficulty in getting an acquittal without even the jury having to retire. Publicly the case was over.

The acquittal was popular both in Society and in Parliament and the case did Melbourne's reputation little of the harm which would have been done to that of a modern Prime Minister in a similar predicament. His brother, however, commented that he was lucky to have survived two such cases and that he would be wise not to tempt Providence with further indiscretions. That for a man in his position his conduct had been indiscreet is plain, but Melbourne was never one to care much for public opinion where his personal affairs were concerned. Whether he was in fact guilty of adultery is something on which there can be no final certainty. Caroline denied it consistently and so did he, and there is no evidence except opportunity to suggest that they were lying. An emotional friendship would probably most accurately describe their relationship. Between a beautiful woman and an older, experienced and attractive man, some element of a flirtatious nature can give edge and spice to their friendship, and emotion as well as affection in their companionship there most certainly was. Though for a time it was not expedient for them to resume their friendship, after his resignation in 1841 for the remainder of his life they both wrote and visited one another and in his will he asked his brother to make some provision for her while she continued to fight to have access to her children and to protect herself against a legal system that regarded her as her husband's chattel, incapable legally of keeping even the money that she earned by her pen. But in 1836 no longer could Melbourne drop in at Storey's Gate on the way back from Parliament. He had either to rely on other friends or return to a quiet home. This became even more so when in November his son Augustus, whose birth had caused so much joy both to him and Lady Caroline, and whose mental retardment had cast such a shadow over both his parents, died quite quietly, life merely flickering out. While he lived Melbourne had someone for whom to care, even if he had long given up any hope that his son might live a full and normal life. Now there was no one left except old friends and political colleagues; even Emily Eden was in India, where her brother was Governor General. Another chapter of his frustrating life had closed. He could not then have guessed that with the death of William IV and the accession of the young Victoria in 1837 he was again to find purpose, affection and fulfilment.

8

VICTORIA: THE YEARS
OF FULFILMENT

VICTORIA was only just eighteen when she became Queen of England. In her own much-quoted words she was 'perhaps in many ways though not in all things, inexperienced'. She had had a difficult childhood. Her mother, the Duchess of Kent, had been over-protective, over-possessive and completely under the influence of the Comptroller of her Household, Sir John Conroy, who aimed to use that influence to make himself the power behind the throne on Victoria's accession, either by securing the Regency for the Duchess until her daughter became twenty-one, or by forcing the young princess to bind herself formally and in writing to appoint him as her private secretary. In the months preceding the late King's death Victoria had been subjected to intensive pressure to force her to sign away her freedom of action. She had not succumbed but the experience had been one that had toughened and disciplined a naturally affectionate and impulsive disposition. She had learnt to withstand pressure; she had learnt to keep her own counsel. She had accustomed herself – and this may have been a more dangerous lesson – to identify her own will with the rights and privileges of the Crown and to feel, half unconsciously, that to oppose the one was to infringe the other. Her inexperience lay with her unfamiliarity with the kind of political problems which as Queen she would have to face. This was largely due to the bitter dislike that existed between William IV and the

Duchess, which had kept Victoria more than ordinarily divorced from the day-to-day life of the Court. As far as it was within his power to do so her uncle, Leopold, King of the Belgians, had endeavoured, by directing her reading and by a series of letters designed to educate his niece for her future responsibilities, to prepare her for her duties as Queen. But despite his sending his confidential adviser, Baron Stockmar, to hold a watching brief when it became clear that the death of William IV was imminent, politically Victoria was in desperate need of wise counsel and steady support when in June 1837 she became Queen. She needed more than an efficient and able Prime Minister; she needed a man who would be constantly at hand, a man who could first awake and then bear the weight of the affection for which this rather lonely and very young woman had hitherto had no emotional outlet. In Lord Melbourne she found a Prime Minister who, possibly of all the active politicians in 1837, could alone have played this dual role. It is fascinating to speculate as to what would have been the results, both for Victoria and the country, had Sir Robert Peel been in office instead of Melbourne. Charles Greville thought 'it foortunate that she had fallen into his hands, and that he will discharge this great duty wisely, honourably and conscientiously'. He had no doubts that Melbourne was 'both equal to and worthy of the task'.

From their first meeting, when at nine o'clock on the morning of 20 June the Prime Minister, handsome and resplendent in full court dress, came to kiss his new sovereign's hand, this was her own reaction. Acting on her uncle's advice she then informed him that she intended to make no changes in her government, whereupon he kissed hands again formally as her minister. Their first impressions of each other were favourable. In her diary that night Victoria declared that she liked him very much and had confidence in him, describing him with all her favourite and most laudatory adjectives: he was straightforward, clever, honest and good. By the time she made her entry she had already had some grounds for her judgement. There had been much public business to discuss, including the first meeting of the Privy Council, and by the time that they had their final conversation together after dinner on that first momentous day Victoria was already feeling comfortable with him. He for his part told Lord Lansdowne that 'nothing could be more proper and feeling than her behaviour'. It was an auspicious beginning. Further acquaintance was to show how mutual the attraction between them was. By July the Queen was congratulating herself on having some-one at the head of her government in whom she had such complete confidence, writing that 'there are not many like him in this world of deceit'. By the middle of the month in the pages of her diary he had become 'my friend', a title emphasised by her emphatic underlining. For his part Melbourne, who, as Greville pointed out, was 'not a man to be easily captivated or dazzled by any superficial accomplishments or mere graces of manner, or even personal favour', thought highly of her sense, discretion and good feeling. His response to her need of him was as spontaneous and instinctive as his need of her. Greville, who had known him for a long time, perceptively described him as 'a man with a capacity for loving without having anything in the world to love'. Now, with unexpected generosity, Fate had given him the opportunity to 'educate, instruct and form the most interesting mind and character in the world', interesting not so much because of her innate qualities as because she was an inexperienced ruling Queen. For him Greville thought 'no occupation could be more engrossing' and by September the diarist had no doubt that Melbourne was as 'passionately fond of her as he might be of a daughter'.

It is not surprising that Victoria fell so completely under his charm. His good looks had been notorious as a young man and even now, though a little portly and with his dark hair turning grey, Fanny Kemble described him as 'exceedingly handsome, with a fine person, verging towards the portly, and a sweet countenance, more expressive of refined careless good humour than almost any face I ever saw. His beauty was too well born and bred a type to be unpleasantly sensual; but his whole face, person expression and manner conveyed the idea of a pleasure-loving nature, habitually self-indulgent and indulgent to others. He was my beau ideal of an Epicurean philosopher (supposing it possible that an Epicurean philosopher could have consented to become Prime Minister of England.).' Victoria was always particularly susceptible to good looks in a man – witness her reaction to Albert – but there were far more solid grounds for her devotion to Melbourne. Her company brought out all that was best in him. No longer carelessly self-indulgent, because it really mattered so little to anyone, he took great pains never to shock or to frighten her. Again and again she recorded instances of his gentleness and of the patience with which he explained the problems on which, as Queen, she would have to make a decision; he was such a complete contrast to Sir John Conroy with his bullying techniques. Moreover Lord Melbourne never made her feel stupid. It did not take him long to discover both the strength and the limits of her mind. Later, when their political partnership had been finally shattered by the fall of the Whigs in 1841, approaching Greville in his usual casual way he asked him 'Have you any means of speaking to these chaps? I think there are one or two things Peel ought to be told, and I wish you would tell him. Don't let him suffer any appointment he is going to make to be talked about, and don't let her hear about it through anybody but himself; and whenever he does anything, or has anything to propose, let him explain to her clearly his reasons. The Queen is not conceited; she is aware there are many things she cannot understand, and she likes to have them explained to her elementarily, not at length and in detail, but shortly and clearly; neither does she like long audiences, and I never stayed with her a long time.' Such was the fruit of four years' experience of his royal mistress; devoted though she was to Melbourne, when tired or strung up she could administer a sharp reprimand even to him. Delightful though in the main their relations were she was not always an easy person with whom to work, though in general she was genuinely penitent when she had made him suffer from her moods.

Much of what in these four years he did to 'educate and instruct' he did not as her Prime Minister but as her secretary and confidential friend. Because of the difficulty of finding the right person to act in the latter capacity he took these secretarial duties upon himself. When acting as the head of her government he wrote to her with all the formality which he had shown to William IV, when the iron hand of the politician was veiled in the courtly glove of deference. But in their daily conversations he allowed himself more latitude, though Charles Villiers, returning from a visit to Windsor, commented on his manner towards her in what today might be called 'after office hours', describing it as 'so paternal and anxious, but always so respectful and deferential, though, as her diary shows, this did not prevent him teasing her gently in what she called his 'funny' way. In consequence it became more and more necessary for her comfort and peace of mind to have him near her. On public occasions, such as the opening of Parliament, and even more on that grand occasion of her coronation, this gave her a sense of security. In her own account of that unique occasion, she wrote: 'when my good Lord Melbourne knelt down and kissed my hand, he pressed my hand and I grasped his with all my heart, at which he looked up with his eyes filled with tears and seemed much touched, as he was, I observed throughout the whole ceremony.' One of the moments that moved him deeply was when the crown was placed on Victoria's head, followed simultaneously by the peers and peeresses putting on their own coronets. Both his concern and his pride were understandable; by then each was possibly the most important person in the other's life. This was certainly true of Melbourne who was too skilful to seem to challenge, or rival, Victoria's two other emotional attachments, the Baroness Lehzen and the King of the Belgians. On 4 June Lehzen was still her 'dearest friend' and by 1 November Melbourne too was being described as 'being a great friend of Lehzen's which' she added, 'makes me *more* fond of him still'; an ingenuous comment which might not have come as a complete surprise to Lord Melbourne. He was equally successful with the King of the Belgians when the latter and his wife came to stay at Windsor, though this success was probably less hardly earned then the regard of the somewhat unattractive Baroness, because according to Victoria, he and her beloved uncle shared the same views on politics.

By the autumn Melbourne had become a constant visitor at Windsor. Victoria tended to be possessive with the people whom she loved; Melbourne had become necessary to her and if for any reason he had to remain in London while she was at Windsor she was very conscious of that gap that his absence created. Life at the court followed a fixed pattern, one which Charles Greville, on a brief visit described as: 'The Queen gets up at eight, breakfasts in her room, then gets down to business, reads dispatches etc. At eleven or twelve Melbourne comes and stays an hour or so. At two she rides out with a large suite, Melbourne always rides at her left hand. Amuses herself for the rest of the afternoon. Dinner nominally at 7.30 but she rarely appears before eight.' Melbourne always sat next to the Queen

who was 'continually talking to him', and though the ladies
retired as convention demanded, leaving the men, Victoria
rarely left them to enjoy the unrestrained masculine atmosphere
for more than a quarter of an hour before summoning them to
coffee. After coffee the party then adjourned to the drawing
room where, again in Greville's words, The Queen 'sits at a
large round table, her guests around it, and Melbourne always
on a chair beside her, where two mortal hours are consumed in
such conversation as can be found, which appears to be, and
really is, very uphill work'. Plainly Greville was bored but these
evenings, as seen through the Queen's own eyes, were quite
delightful. Sometimes she varied the procedure by sitting on the
sofa with some favoured female guest beside her but with Lord
Melbourne always sitting near. It was at these evening sessions
that he was able to do so much to 'educate and instruct' the
young Queen whose education, though not precisely inadequate,
had been limited and formal. No one was better fitted for this
task than Melbourne, who was able to put her at her ease 'by his
frank and natural manners while he amuses her by the quaint
queer epigrammatic turn of his mind and his varied knowledge
upon all subjects.' He had always been an amusing
conversationalist, making outrageous statements so that it was
difficult to know whether the opinions that, in Victoria's words,
he expounded 'so funnily' were his own or said merely for
effect. When he grew excited he would pull his hair with a
boyishness that she found most endearing and she was for ever
commenting on his 'blunt amusing manner of coming out with
his remarks and observations'. They talked about everything
under the sun from the punishment of children to the
difficulties of Henry VIII, with whom Melbourne declared
himself disposed to sympathise. Victoria was an enthusiastic
play-goer, which gave rise to numerous discusssions on the
various plays of Shakespeare. Melbourne conceded that *Lear*
was a fine play but personally he confessed that he found the
madness scenes repugnant and Lear himself a foolish old fellow.
He also found the end of *Hamlet* 'horrid and awkward'. Music
provided a less common interest; to Victoria it was one of the
highest pleasures but to Melbourne it was comparatively
unexplored ground. When he was young, he told her, he and his
set had affected to despise both music and dancing, preferring
to lounge on sofas, and in consequence he had never cultivated a

taste for music though he rather preened himself on his appreciation of art, as indeed anyone familiar with Petworth had every right to do. They discussed literature; Scott's novels he commended, though he disliked Dickens with his mass of squalid details about low life. He had also little good to say of women writers, which perhaps, in view of the anguish caused to all the Lambs by *Glenarvon*, is not surprising. History of every kind was a perennial topic. Here he was particularly well equipped both to direct her reading and to bring the more immediate past to life with anecdotes of the people he had known either first hand or *via* the recollections of his older friends.

Not all their conversations were on serious and improving topics. He was at once too clever and too gay for that. He discoursed wittily on Paris bonnets, and the Queen found him 'funny and nice about toilette'. He noticed when she wore a new dress, or altered her hair style or wore more or less jewellery and Victoria thought his taste in such matters good, though even here she made her own decisions, which were not always those of which his taste approved. In the main, though, he added just enough criticisms to give authenticity to his approval. In the three years before her marriage there was little, serious or trivial, that they did not discuss: people, horses, dogs, actors and actresses, the unwisdom of early marriages, wife beating, the middle classes, education, the poor, trade unions, the past and the present. Inevitably, for good or ill these conversations were to influence Victoria's mind and outlook, occurring as they did when she was at a most impressionable age. She was eagerly appreciative at the time of everything that fell from his lips, conscious of how much she was gaining from them, and when he was absent, as sometimes he unavoidably was, she missed him. Greville wondered how he contrived to survive the double strain of political leadership and royal bear leading, though he did not put it in quite those words. What he wrote was that it was 'marvellous that he should be able to overcome the force of habit so completely as to endure the life he leads. Month after month he remains at the Castle, submitting to the daily routine; of all men he appeared to be the last to be broken in to the trammels of a Court, and never was such a revolution seen in anybody's occupation and habits. Instead of indolently sprawling in all the attitudes of luxurious ease, he is always sitting bolt upright; his free and easy language, interlarded with "damns" is carefully guarded and regulated with the strictest propriety, and he has exchanged the good talk of Holland House for the trivial, laboured and wearisome inanities of the Royal Circle'. His contemporaries regarded Melbourne as charming, casual, amusing and indolent; what was not so clearly seen was that when faced with some task that he thought worth the effort he could be as self-disciplined and industrious as any dedicated man. As a Prime Minister his methods might appear easy going but he did in fact get through a great deal of detailed adminstrative business. As he once told Victoria he could always find time to do what must be done, it was only the inessentials that were put off from day to day. Greville was more perceptive in realising that the elderly statesman and the young Queen were becoming too interdependent, particularly when the Court was at Windsor, writing 'she really has nothing to do with anyone but Melbourne and with him she passes (if not tête à tête yet in intimate communication) more hours than any two people, in any relation of life, perhaps ever do pass together. He is at her side for at least six hours every day – an hour in the morning, two on horse back, one at dinner and two in the evening.'

There is no doubt that both Melbourne and the Queen found deep personal happiness in this relationship but Greville was prophetic in seeing squalls ahead in spite of what in his opinion was Melbourne's 'discretion and purity of conduct and behaviour, which made him admired, respected and liked by all the Court', in itself no mean tribute to a man known to monopolise Court favour. His personal standing with the Crown was unchallenged; his political position was not. The election held after Victoria's accession had weakened still further the Whig core of the ministry, leaving it more than ever dependent on the Radical and Irish vote. An adverse vote in the Commons meant that Melbourne would be forced to resign and would then be replaced by the Tory Sir Robert Peel. When this happened, inevitably he saw that 'the parting will be painful, and their subsequent relations will not be without embarrassment to themselves, nor fail to be a cause of jealousy in others'. The Queen herself was acutely conscious that the continuance of their unrestricted communication depended neither on her nor on Lord Melbourne but on a continuance of a Whig majority in the Commons and her attitude was thoroughly partisan. She was prepared to support the Whigs, as her conduct over the Bedchamber question was to demonstrate, to the limits of her constitutional authority and beyond it. The occasion of a critical vote on the Irish Church question in May 1838 was responsible for the rather youthfully touching entry in her diary to the effect that 'I trust fervently that He who has so wonderfully protected me through such manifold difficulties will not *now* desert me.' Throughout her life Victoria had the comforting conviction that the Almighty took the same view of the problems that confronted her as she did and she could never quite understand why sometimes He acted so strangely in the ordering of events. Greville had been right to stress the personal and political problems that her reliance on Lord Melbourne must cause at some future date when the mere possibility that he might be defeated in the Commons was so distressing that she feared she would choke with tears if she even discussed it with him.

Melbourne's political difficulties remained the same, though intensified by his declining majority in the Commons. In the Lords he was under constant attack by Brougham and Lord Lyndhurst, who in 1836 had distinguished himself by making a bitter onslaught on the Prime Minister for failing to resign when unable to carry his policy in that House. In former times, he thundered, 'amid such disasters there was only one course for a minister to pursue. These however were antiquated notions. A fastidious delicacy formed no part of the character of the noble Viscount. He told them that, notwithstanding the insubordinate temper of his crew, he would stick to the vessel while a single plank remained afloat. But, as a friendly adviser, he would recommend him to get as speedily as possible into still water.' This, while he still had a reasonable majority behind him in the Commons, Melbourne simply refused to do, declaring, 'I conscientiously believe that the well-being of the country requires in the judgment of the people that I shall hold my present office - and hold it I will - until I am removed.' After 1837 he had an additional reason for holding on: Victoria's reliance on him. As the Lords continued to throw out bills approved by the Lower House an observer as acute as Macaulay thought the Lords were on a dangerous collision course, believing 'the probability is that popular opinion will gather strength every year. In the meantime the Lords are becoming fiercer and more obstinate every day. The young aristocrats who are destined to fill the seats of the present peers are even more bigoted than their fathers.' His personal assessment was that the hold on popular imagination of the hereditary aristocracy, which had formerly been so strong, was declining and that in consequence there would be a showdown within a generation. In this he was wrong. Nevertheless as a piece of political prophesy his diagnosis is interesting, as is also the query as to what part the long reign of Victoria played in delaying the subordination of the House of Lords until the Parliament Act of 1912. Modern readers are inclined to forget the revolutionary urges, the questioning and the discontent that were an integral part of political thinking in the Great Britain over whose administration Lord Melbourne presided.

Lord John Russell, very conscious of the weakness of the government's position and more radical in his views than Melbourne, suggested strengthening the administration by taking in Lord Durham, but this he refused to do even though his position was made still more difficult by the threat of an economic recession. By 1837 it was clear that the prosperity of the last few years was petering out. Unemployment was growing precisely at a time when the Poor Law Commissioners were determined to enforce the new and hated Poor Law Amendment Act of 1834, with its detested union workhouses, in the industrial north, having previously concentrated their efforts against the apparently more pauperised rural areas of the south. The result was widespread resistance with its threat to law and order combined with a declining revenue when, in the absence of an income tax, so much of it came from the indirect taxation that depended on demand. It is unfair to charge Melbourne with a failure to realise that the prosperity of the last few years was over; he was more aware of the onset of a period of financial stringency than some of his colleagues. But he had no aptitude for dealing with such issues and there was no outstanding man in his Cabinet who could supply his deficiencies. That the leader of the Opposition, Sir Robert Peel, was such a man did nōt help the Whigs who in comparison were so badly supplied with the statistics that Peel used with such effect in his speeches that Melbourne's brother Fred, now created Lord Beauvale, asked acidly why government departments could not be instructed to supply the Prime

Minister with similar material, arguing that to rely on mere clerks and copyists to furnish the kind of information that such difficult controversial questions required was totally inadequate.

One such question which was being increasingly raised was that of the Corn Laws. In the interests of the landed classes free trade in corn had always been prohibited and in 1837 import was regulated by a sliding scale that fell as prices rose. To the industrialists of the north such protection was anathema; it put up the price of food and discouraged foreigners from buying British goods when these could not be paid for by exporting corn to Britain. The problem was an intricate one and cannot be discussed here. Nevertheless it generated a great deal of heat and Lord John grew more attracted to the idea of a moderate fixed duty instead of a sliding scale. Melbourne disliked the whole idea and differences on this subject between him and the Radicals did nothing to contribute to the stability of the administration.

If Melbourne was unfitted to deal with such problems he was equally insensitive to the fact that the wind of change was also blowing in British possessions overseas, and particularly in Canada. Melbourne, like most of his generation, was not imperially minded; the independence of America, secured in 1783, had left an enormous hole in the old empire while the potential of Australia and Canada had been grasped by only a few, among whom Melbourne could not be numbered. Nor was Lord Glenelg, the Colonial Secretary, the man to handle thorny problems with the requisite mixture of imagination and firmness that the situation required. By the December of 1837 Lord Howick was urging the Prime Minister either to replace Glenelg or himself to 'assume the management of this Canadian business', writing firmly that 'you ought much sooner to have given your serious attention to the affairs of the colony', and entreating him 'to rouse yourself from your past inaction, to make yourself really master of the facts'. This Melbourne failed to do, faced as he was with a hostile House of Lords that was blocking all government measures until ministers were prepared to drop the appropriation clauses in dealing with the Irish Church, and engrossed in the needs of the young Queen. His hand was finally forced when early in 1838 rebellion broke out in Canada, which by then had outgrown the constitutional arrangements made for its government when the province had been sparsely populated, largely by settlers of French origin. The end of the American War of Independence had seen a considerable influx of Empire loyalists, and subsequently in the nineteenth century of fresh emigrants from Britain, bringing with them demands for a greater degree of self-government. The result was discontent and growing friction between the French, largely concentrated in Lower Canada round Montreal and Quebec, and the British in Upper Canada. The rebellion in Lower Canada was completely put down by Sir John Colborne, and a subsequent one in Upper Canada by its Governor, Sir Francis Head, but it was clear that the Canadian question could be shelved no longer. Legislation to meet the immediate emergency was thrashed out in a divided Cabinet, and because of a general lack of confidence in Lord Glenelg's ability to handle the situation it was decided to send out a Governor General with special powers. Unexpectedly Melbourne chose Lord Durham for this mission. Melbourne had no liking for him and it may have been a temptation to get him out of the way, but superficially, though vain and theatrical, Durham had some genuine qualifications. He was reputed able, he was progressive and popular with the Radicals, a fact which if he were forced to take strong measures in Canada might blunt their criticism. When Victoria gave him an audience on 28 January 1838 he impressed her with his grasp of Canadian issues and clearly she saw no reason to share either Melbourne's dislike or distrust of the man. If something had to be done for Durham, to keep him fully employed on the other side of the Atlantic seemed a viable solution.

Nevertheless for Melbourne it proved a bad appointment; Durham showed an independence and insubordination that was to make life difficult for the already weak administration. Later, with hindsight, Greville declared that 'The Ministers ought never to have sent him knowing what he was.' It is easy to be wise after the event. The first sign of trouble was when Durham, on arriving in Canada, appointed Thomas Turton as one of his private secretaries and a member of his executive council. It was not Turton's abilities that were in question but his morals; he had been engaged in a very sordid affair with his sister-in-law. Lord Wharncliffe promptly raised the matter in the Lords and on 2 July Melbourne wrote to Durham in some distress, complaining of the embarrassing position in which Durham's action had placed him. On 17 July he wrote again reiterating that 'It will do you much harm, it will do me much harm', adding ruefully that the appointment was 'one of those gratuitous and unnecessary difficulties which men most unaccountably create for themselves and which are generally greater than any that are created for them by the natural course of events'. Next day he wrote again in fresh alarm after the question had been asked whether the appointment of Turton were the prelude to a similar appointment for Gibbon Wakefield. Once again the stumbling block was morals. Durham could hardly have picked a man better qualified to help him sort out the tangle of Canadian affairs but Wakefield had spent three years in prison for having abducted an heiress and Melbourne now wrote in haste to warn Durham that if Wakefield were given an official post 'No power on earth could prevent an address to remove both him and Mr Turton from being moved and carried in the House of Lords, and I believe in the House of Commons', adding bitterly: 'It is incredible that a man of common sense should show such an ignorance, or such a disregard of public feeling and opinion as you have done in the selection of these gentlemen.' Worse was to follow. One of the outstanding questions left for Durham's decision was what should be done with the prisoners responsible for the late rebellion. Durham's solution was sensible, even humane, but not legal in that it was beyond the power of his commission. By an ordinand, which was in fact *ultra vires,* he ordered those already in his hands to be deported to the Bahamas, while those who had fled he sentenced to death should they return.

Once again Melbourne had to face the backlash in the Lords, where Brougham and Lyndhurst put him in the humiliating position of having to accept an act indemnifying Durham, which was a clear and public acknowledgement that the Queen's chosen representative in Canada had acted illegally. Many people, including Durham himself, thought Melbourne's defending speech in the debate half-hearted but, as he emphasised in a letter to Durham on 19 August, the latter had made any defence of the ordinance more difficult through his own failure to supply ministers with the relevant details. It is an interesting study in personal relations between two men of very different outlooks. By 26 October Melbourne was confessing that 'I dislike him so much, that there is no course that would please me so well as setting him at defiance', while Durham resented most bitterly the failure of the ministry to support him and his Canadian policy. The rest of the story belongs to Canada's history and is too involved to detail here. Finally, as his last insubordinate act, Durham issued a proclamation in Canada voicing his criticisms of the Home Government, flung up his appointment and returned home in high dudgeon to write, with the massive assistance of Wakefield, the famous Durham report, so influential in shaping subsequent constitutional development in that colony. For Canada Durham's Governor Generalship was both momentous and largely beneficial but Melbourne's position appeared more precarious than ever as Lord John was now threatening to resign if Lord Glenelg was left at the Colonial Office any longer. To prevent any such breakup of the administration Melbourne finally secured a reluctant resignation from Glenelg and replaced him at the Colonial Office by Lord Normanby. Victoria commented that it was 'very wrong' of Lord John Russell and Lord Howick, another malcontent, to have caused Melbourne so much trouble. In this respect she was not guiltless herself, as when the move finally took place she rebuked him for not having kept her as fully informed as she considered it her right to be. For a little longer the weakened and divided adminstration was to totter on.

Not all Melbourne's troubles were political. In 1838 the Queen appeared more capricious and demanding, as her touchiness over Normanby's appointment demonstrated. She was suffering from the very natural reaction from the excitement of the last few months. She was after all only eighteen, a fact that it is easy to forget in the face of her self-possession and dignity. Moreover, affectionate and gay as she was, there was a darker side to her character, a power of resentment forged by the earlier dominance of Conroy and of the Duchess her mother. In public, appearances were kept up, but in her private life Victoria had neither forgiven nor forgotten, and included in her bitterness was anyone connected with this past. It was because of her own resentment towards Conroy and her mother that Victoria, abetted by her old governess Lehzen, was so credulously prepared to accept a scandalous explanation of a change that they both noticed in Lady Flora Hastings' figure when she returned to Court after having visited her family in Scotland.Victoria had never cared for Lady Flora, who was one of her mother's ladies in waiting and was therefore very willing to think ill of her, so that the fact that the suspicious swelling should have occurred after Lady Flora had travelled south in the company of Sir John Conroy seemed to imply the possibility that she might be pregnant. Lady Flora had in fact been feeling unwell in December before travelling north and had consulted Sir James Clark, who was physician both to the Queen and to her mother, but he had not thought her indisposition serious and there was no reason why Victoria should have heard about it. Consequently neither she nor Lehzen had any difficulty in convincing themselves that Lady Flora was with child. The next stage in the drama is obscure; somehow their suspicions, possibly shared by now by Sir James Clark, who had only carried out a very cursory diagnosis of Lady Flora's indisposition, gave rise to rumours. Very quickly the Court became a hotbed of gossip. Later Greville criticised Melbourne for his maladroit handling of what soom became a public scandal. 'It is inconceivable' he wrote 'how Melbourne can ever have permitted this disgraceful mischievous scandal, which cannot fail to lower the character of the Court in the eyes of the world. There may be objections to Melbourne's extraordinary domiciliation in the palace; but the compensation ought to have been found in his good sense and experience preventing the possibility of such transactions.' Melbourne, like the Queen, was the victim of his own background and character. Officially as Prime Minister he was first informed of what privately he must have known by Lady Tavistock when she went into waiting at the end of January 1839. Characteristically Melbourne advised waiting but did take the step of consulting Sir James, who declared his inability to give a positive opinion as to Lady Flora's condition. Melbourne hated to take decisions until forced to do so and at this stage he probably believed that Lady Flora was pregnant and that time would justify the gossip. It was not an unsurprising conclusion to which to come. His family background had made him sceptical of female virtue: neither his mother, his sister nor his mother-in-law had been faithful wives. Moreover it would have been difficult for him not to have been influenced by the hard line taken by Victoria and Lehzen when the matter was discussed. So the gossip continued until Lady

Portman came into waiting in mid-February. She, with commendable commonsense, informed the Duchess of the gossip and told Sir James that he must confront Lady Flora with thtthe situation. After some indecision Lady Flora, in order to clear her name, consented to a medical examination by Sir James himself and his colleague Sir Charles Clarke, a specialist in women's diseases. The result of the examination was to prove that Lady Flora was a virgin.

This should have been the end of the matter. The Queen was shocked by the results of her malicious suspicions and arranged to see the injured lady to express her regrets. Unfortunately Lady Flora was so shattered by the experience that the interview could not take place immediately. Meanwhile the doctors themselves in an interview with Melbourne told him that they still had their doubts, because though technically a virgin it was not physically completely impossible that Lady Flora might be pregnant. Melbourne may well have believed this to be true. When therefore the Queen saw Lady Flora on 23 February, unfortunately by then family feeling had been aroused. Lord Hastings, Lady Flora's brother, took up his sister's cause, demanding to know who first had spread these malicious rumours. The tension heightened when the Duchess promptly dismissed Sir James from her service, while the Queen withstood all pressure to make her do likewise. Melbourne appeared quite unable to control the situation and by March the press was giving publicity to the whole affair. Wellington tried, unsuccessfully, to calm down the feelings both of the Hastings family and of the Court and finally the bombshell exploded. The much tried Lady Flora had written to her uncle a full account of all that she had suffered, and on 17 March her letter was published in *The Examiner*. It was no longer a question of a personal vendetta; the issue had become political. The Hastings were Tories and the Tories rallied behind them to attack the government. Melbourne was actually beaten on a motion in the House of Lords by five votes. It seemed as if the fate of the ministry hung in the balance, for though the motion was on Ireland and not ostensibly linked to the Hastings affair, it was that which had destroyed the government's credit and reputation. However, after a full Cabinet meeting, the Prime Minister decided not to resign while he still had the confidence of the Crown and the Commons where, after the Easter recess, a motion moved by Lord John Russell approving their recent policy in Ireland was carried by 318 to 296.

The respite was short. By May the Government were again in trouble, this time over Jamaica. Slavery had been abolished in all the British colonies by the Whig government but, partly to ease thtthe period of transition for the slave-owners, a system of apprenticeship was instituted, which gave them considerable control, including the right to flog their negro workers, over their erstwhile slaves. This was ended in 1838, two years earlier than had been originally intended, and the result in Jamaica had been considerable unrest and defiance by the ex-slave owners. Finally Melbourne's government decided that it was necessary to suspend the Jamaican constitution, as had previously been done after the Canadian rebellion. The Radicals disliked what they regarded as an attack on constitutional liberties and Peel seized the opportunity to launch his own political offensive in the Commons. There the government majority sank to five and, already in a permanent minority in the Lords, it was clear that Melbourne could no longer carry on. Lord John Russell was therefore sent to break the news to the Queen that the Cabinet had decided to resign. In the afternoon Melbourne came himself. It was an affecting interview, with Victoria in 'a dreadful state of grief' and he telling her sadly, when he wrote to her afterwards that 'nothing had ever given him so much pain.' In spite of his own sorrow, both for her and for himself, he behaved with complete constitutional propriety, breaking it to the almost distraught Victoria that he could not continue to be received by her while negotiations with the Tories were still going on and advising her to send for Peel. It seemed the end of the road; Victoria was to lose her 'excellent Lord Melbourne' who for the past two years had been almost a father to her, and he was to be exiled at once from power and from the palace. The former he could face with equanimity, since for months he had been aware that the burden of his responsibilities was greater than his strength to bear them, but to be bereft of Victoria's company, difficult and exhausting as he had often found her demands on him, he knew would leave an unfillable gap in his emotional life. Once again, in spite of his family and old friends, he would be alone, his pattern of living in ruins and the future an uncertain grey. If it was difficult for Victoria to face the future without his tender affection and experience to sustain her, she at least had the resilience of youth to support her; he could only stand by, rendered helpless by constitutional usage to help her when she most needed the reassurance of his presence. The fact that, as Lady Palmerston reported, the Queen was in tears and miserable and could not appear at dinner can have done little to comfort him.

9

SUNSET AND TWILIGHT

AGAINST all reasonable expectations Melbourne, who resigned on 7 May, was back in office by the 11th. The person most responsible for this political *volte face* was the Queen herself, though a suggestion on the part of Lord Melbourne on resigning that she had better express the hope to Peel that none of her Household, except those actively engaged in politics, should be removed, was in part responsible. Victoria at the outset of her negotiation with Wellington, whom she preferred, and Peel, whom she disliked, had every intention of behaving with constitutional propriety. Though the atmosphere was not cordial it was correct and the negotiations appeared to be going smoothly until the question of the Household came up. The Queen was known to be an ardent Whig and it is understandable that Peel should want some public display of her confidence in him. Moreover he could hardly have been happy to leave the Queen surrounded by 'Ladies' such as Lady Normanby, the wife of one of the leading ex-ministers, in spite of Victoria's assurance that she never talked politics with her Ladies. On her part the Queen considered any attempt to interfere with them as a gross infringement of her personal freedom, A solution was the more difficult to discover because there was no precedent to act as a guide. The last reigning woman sovereign was Queen Anne, and at the beginning of the eighteenth century the political set-up was completely different, as far as the royal

143

power was concerned, from that of 1839. Victoria therefore refused to give up any of her Ladies and Peel told her that without some proof of her confidence he and his colleagues felt they could not form a government. At her request Melbourne came to see her on the 9th and, as a result of a long conversation, he called a meeting of the Cabinet to discuss this new situation. After a lengthy meeting and much discussion it was decided that they should advise the Queen to inform Sir Robert Peel that she could not consent to the removal of the Ladies of the Bedchamber. As to what had actually taken place between the Queen and Sir Robert in the decisive interview there is some confusion. Victoria certainly gave Lord Melbourne, and through him the Cabinet, to understand that Peel had intended to remove *all* the Ladies whereas in his subsequent written reply Peel revealed that he had only spoken of 'some changes'. When Melbourne realised this, even Victoria could see that he was shaken. To the indignant young Queen there might be very little difference between 'some' and 'all' but to an experienced politician the two were by no means the same thing and he insisted that these new facts must be put before the Cabinet. Victoria got the support that she wanted and Peel refused to take office on her terms. It was an emotional rather than a constitutional decision. Melbourne told a friend that 'I resume office solely because I will not abandon my sovereign in a state of difficulty and distress.'

Victoria was exultant. People noticed how happy she seemed at the Duchess of Gloucester's ball and on the 12th the familiar entry appeared in her journal: 'Lord Melbourne sitting near me'. His own feelings must have been more mixed. Victoria described him as being very excited the whole evening, talking to himself, which was a habit he had developed, and pulling his hair about. Undoubtedly his devotion to Victoria must have made the prospect of losing his close intimacy a bleak one and the spectacle of her distress must have augmented his with the knowledge that it was now out of his power to mitigate it. But there was another side. The strain of office was beginning to tell on his once magnificent vitality, and that, combined with consistent overindulgence, particularly in food, was affecting his health. In a moment of weariness he once confessed to Victoria that whereas when a young man he had not known what it was to feel ill, now he never felt quite well. Victoria worried about his health and her journal contains repeated comments on it; he could not attend the Queen because he was unwell; he looked tired; he was apt to drop asleep after dinner, which she believed was always a sign that he was not 'quite well' though he defended himself by saying in his exaggerated way that everyone should lie round the room after dinner and sleep. The defence revealed his inner exhaustion; Lady Caroline's husband would have thought it a very odd way indeed of passing the evening. When Victoria thought he looked very well or in high spirits she rejoiced. It was not only the Queen who was concerned about his health. Both his sister Emily, now Lady Palmerston, and his brother Fred were also worried. Emily indeed declared that in her opinion ministers should be paid at an extra rate like workmen in an unhealthy trade because of the constant overwork and worry that office involved, while Fred lamented that William was once again in office, declaring that when the Whigs had been forced to resign he thought his brother well out of it, whereas now his position would be 'full of thorns' and that 'No human strength can go on session after session without breaking down.'

Meanwhile the political situation was, if anything, still more precarious. Though the immediate reaction of the crowd was to support the Queen against what was represented as the bullying attitude of the Tories, there were still rumblings from the Lady Flora affair. When she drove up the course at Ascot with Melbourne they were hissed by a couple of Lady Flora's friends and when, early in July, that unfortunate woman died and a post mortem showed the cause of death to have been a malignant growth on the liver the whole miserable business once again became a matter for recrimination, which the fact that Victoria had visited Lady Flora shortly before her death and had sent a carriage to represent her at the funeral did little to lessen. Sir James Clark's reputation was torn to shreds by his detractors and the failure of the Queen to dismiss him involved her afresh in a wave of unpopularity. Her nerves were torn to pieces and much of the gaiety and high spirits that had made her such a delightful companion gave way to easy irritation. If the affair of Lady Flora had created a clique hostile to the Queen in London society, economic depression was fostering radical discontent in the country as a whole. The euphoria of the Reform Act had long since passed away. Since the latter months of 1836 Britain

145

had been increasingly in the grip of a depression and both then and in the following years there was widespread unemployment, particularly in Lancashire and the Midlands. There were serious riots and a general defiance of the law in northern towns when attempts were made to enforce the hated Poor Law. The Chartist movement grew out of this general mood of disillusion and men who now would be described as 'left wing' working-class leaders began to demand a further instalment of parliamentary reform sufficiently radical to give them overwhelming representation in the House of Commons. This was to be achieved through manhood suffrage, the abolition of the property qualification for members, who were to be paid, equal electoral districts and – to insure that the Commons and the people did not get out of step – annual Parliaments. These demands were contained in a document known as *The Charter* and men holding such views were therefore known as Chartists. Throughout 1837 and 1838 there were demonstrations and rallies in all parts of the country, culminating in the calling of a People's Convention which met in London in February to draw up a monster petition that was to be presented to Parliament. In the event this proved to be something of a damp squib: the Chartist movement was hopelessly divided between its more moderate and its extreme sections, each fighting for control, and was more a bundle of local parties, each with its own individual interests, than a unified national campaign. But to the authorities it held dangerous revolutionary potential and provided an uneasy background of social discontent when the Government itself was tottering over the Bedchamber crisis. In the Commons the Charter had few adherents and in July a motion moved by the radical Thomas Attwood that the House should consider the petition was defeated by 235 votes to 46. In spite of the publicity that the Charter received none of the riots reached dangerous proportions and Lord John, as Home Secretary, kept the situation well in hand.

The radicals within the Commons represented a greater danger because the Whigs depended on them to maintain their majority and were themselves divided on the best policy to adopt in face of these demands. One instance will suffice as an illustration of the tensions that perpetually harassed Melbourne. In June 1839 Sir Hesketh Fleetwood decided to move a motion to extend the £10 borough franchise to the counties and Lord John wanted to conciliate the Radicals by considering it, while Lord Howick, backed by his father Lord Grey, was utterly opposed to any alteration in the Reform Act associated with his name, which Melbourne told Victoria had annoyed Lord John very much. Finally in a Cabinet meeting it was decided that Lord John should say that the Government were prepared to consider the proposal next year, but in the actual debate he said instead that he could hold out no hope of the Government considering the proposal even at a future date. His subsequent explanation for reversing a decision taken by the Cabinet was that with so small a majority behind him, in face of his colleague Lord Howick's threats he dare not do otherwise. Nevertheless on his own responsibility and without consulting Melbourne, he had negated a Cabinet-backed policy and in so doing had alienated the Radicals. Indeed so annoyed were Hobhouse, Normanby and Thompson that they in turn talked of resigning, which Melbourne warned Victoria might bring about a fall of the Government. On this occasion the cracks were papered over and the Radicals soothed by the introduction of the penny post and by agreeing that the issue of the ballot should be regarded as an open question. There was another crisis at the end of the session. Lord John had been pressing for some time to transfer from the Home Office to the Colonial Office and this in turn had led to all kinds of new problems. Melbourne feared that the Commons had no faith in Normanby because of radical opinions, while Howick was so touchy that he was likely to resign. This he eventually did and was replaced by Macaulay, lately returned from India. Again and again Melbourne found himself faced by a divided Cabinet and headstrong colleagues whom it was becoming increasingly difficult to control and whose actions he was forced to defend to a somewhat astringent Victoria. In this manner the Government went on, lurching from crisis to crisis, coping with discontented Irish members and critical Radical ones, and more often more dependent on the goodwill of the Tories than on the enthusiasm of its own supporters. May 1839 had been a reprieve but both Victoria and Melbourne knew that its duration might be short.

Lord Palmerston did little to ease his brother-in-law's path. At the Foreign Office he went his own way, claiming an all but independent empire and shaping foreign policy with little reference to his colleagues, who were frequently forced to accept a *fait accompli* rather than risk his resignation by opposing it. It was not difficult for so forceful a personality to impose his will on a Cabinet divided and weak. Britain's relations with Europe, not yet recovered from the aftermath of the Napoleonic wars, combined with the support given by Metternich to legitimate govenments, presented plenty of problems. There were internal conflicts in Spain and Portugal; the last steps in the creation of an independent Belgium, free from French influence, had to be taken; and the Ottoman empire had already begun the slow process of disintegration that was to make it 'the sick man of Europe'. Palmerston's policy was basically simple. Britain had become a great industrial nation with commercial interests in every part of the globe, even as far east as China. Naval power and the securing of the sea routes to India were of paramount importance. Where British interest were at stake Palmerston was prepared to defend them with a diplomacy backed by naval power even when the British case verged on the dubious. In the matter of Belgian independence, which was finally secured by the Convention of London in 1839, his diplomacy was skilful and successful; the Abolitionists were strongly behind the vigorous use he made of the navy to put down the slave trade; his policy towards the Ottoman empire, however, alarmed and divided the Cabinet. In his view it must be bolstered up in order to prevent Russia having free access to the Mediterranean *via* the Dardanelles. When therefore the Turkish Sultan, against British advice, attacked his over-powerful vassal Mehemet Ali, whose rule since 1833 had extended over both Egypt and Syria, and was decisively beaten, Palmerston was faced with a difficult situation. He could not leave the Turks dependent on Russian help to deal with the victorious Mehemet Ali, nor could he allow the Turkish empire to be weakened drastically by being forced to recognise the independence of both Egypt and Syria. To complicate matters still further the Sultan died and was succeeded by a boy of seventeen. Palmerston's problem therefore was at once to bridle Mehemet Ali by depriving him of Syria and to get the great European Powers as a whole to act together to save the Turks without leaving this to Russia. The negotiations that followed were long and tortuous and in the course of them it looked as if the alliance between France and

Britain, which had been the cornerstone of British diplomacy, would be destroyed. The Cabinet was divided and apprehensive; Melbourne, personally worried and lukewarm towards Palmerston's policy, stressing to the Queen the importance of France co-operating in the plans being worked out for a settlement. One difficulty in this programmme was that France was sympathetic to Mehemet Ali, whom Palmerston therefore feared might be the means by which the French could establish a special position of influence in the Near East, where Britian had considerable trading interests. He therefore threatened to resign if he were not allowed to go ahead with his own handling of the situation and Melbourne, aware that if he did so the Ministry must fall, once again used his considerable powers of conciliation to talk the rest of the Cabinet round, though at one time Lord John, Lord Clarendon and Lord Holland all threatened to resign. It was a tricky and exhausting time for Melbourne, but Palmerston carried his point and by July France had been left out on a limb, though later she returned to the Concert of Europe, thereby vindicating the Foreign Secretary's firmness. When finally the Whigs were defeated in June 1841, dissolved Parliment and, failing to gain a majority at the polls, resigned in September, Palmerston's image alone stood high, in spite of the unpopularity that he had incurred by his support of the opium trade, which was in his eyes merely a means of opening up China to British traders, though it was Peel who garnered the fruits of victory when Hong Kong was ceded to Britain in 1842.

By this time Victoria was no longer as dependent on Melbourne as she had been in 1839, when she had fought so hard to retain him at the head of her government. On 10 February 1840 she had married her cousin Albert of Saxe-Coburg. As in all important instances the decision was her own, though in the preceding year she had discussed all the pros and cons of marriage with Lord Melbourne, the only advantage of marriage in her eyes then being that at least it would free her from the constant presence of her mother the Duchess. Her earlier affection for Albert had become dimmed with time and overlaid by her own role as Queen. She made it very clear to her uncle Leopold, who was pushing the match, that she had no intention of falling in with his scheme for her marriage without first discovering her own feelings when she saw Albert again. At the same time she shrank from that meeting taking place.

Indeed when she discussed the possibility with Melbourne in April 1839 neither of them displayed much enthusiasm for the match. Melbourne stressed the fact that the Coburgs were not popular in Europe and was more than dubious as to the desirability of cousins marrying. This apparently aroused some latent opposition in Victoria. She never could stand contradiction and therefore asked who else there was, stressing the undesirability of marrying a subject. Here Melbourne agreed with her. In the end she asked him if there was any necessity for her marrying at all for the next three or four years. In reply he told her that there seemed little public uneasiness on the matter in spite of the unpopularity of her uncle the King of Hanover, whose machinations were suspected and even feared. The interview closed with a characteristic Melbourne remark. When Victoria confessed that she was doubtful about marrying because she had become so used to getting her own way, he, with an experience based on her capacity in that direction, assured her warmly that she would still do so.

Victoria and Melbourne might procrastinate but her uncle Leopold was not to be put off so easily. He insisted on the visit and on 10 October Albert and his brother Ernest arrived at Windsor. By the 13th the miracle had happened; Victoria was in love and facing the fact that soon she must make up her mind. Melbourne, characteristically, was anxious that she should take another week before doing so, though tactfully he praised Albert's good looks and amiability, and stressed the advantage of his Protestant upbringing. But Victoria knew that she did not need another week. Next day, Monday the 14th, after a rather self-conscious pause, she told Melbourne that she had made her decision; she would marry Albert. When, however, he then began to discuss practical details and suggest a timetable Victoria hesitated to commit herself quite so definitely to marriage and wanted to postpone making an official announcement for at least a year. Lord Melbourne disagreed, knowing how impossible it would be to keep the Queen's engagement a secret. Instead he suggested January, or at the latest February, as the possible date for the marriage. Meanwhile Victoria had still to steel her resolution to tell the Prince himself of her decision to marry. Melbourne urged and she agreed that this should be done as soon as possible and that her uncles Ernest and Leopold, and two leading members of the

Cabinet, Lord John and Lord Palmerston, should also be let into the secret. Throughout their long conversation Victoria was on a knife-edge of emotion, torn between happiness and fear at the seriousness of the step that she was taking, while Melbourne was affectionate and soothing, teasing her gently when she asked his advice on how to put her proposal, and generally acting the part of a devoted father towards a beloved daughter about to leave the nest. Next day she told Albert how happy she would be if he would become her husband, and having crossed her Rubicon turned once again to Melbourne for reassurance. It is clear that she feared entering into any kind of bondage, even that of love, and once again he comforted her, saying that she would in fact be much freer as a married woman to do what she liked.

In the weeks that followed Melbourne's time was tjken up with the practical and often contentious details that the marriage of a reigning Queen entailed. The idea that she should marry was itself popular but there were difficulties connected with her choice of bridegroom. The question of the precedence to be accorded to the husband of the Queen had to be settled, and to her fury Victoria discovered that this was a matter for Parliament. There was also the question of the annuity to be granted by that body to her consort. Prince Leopold, on his marriage to George IV's daughter and heiress, had received £50,000. Some of the chickens of Victoria's Whig partisanship now came home to roost. The Tories were less than co-operative and Melbourne failed to display his usual foresight and tact, perhaps because he saw the approaching marriage so completely through Victoria's eyes that he took too much for granted. The Coburgs had a reputation for doing well for themselves and in 1839 Britain as a whole was far from prosperous, which meant that popular opinion was opposed to making so lavish a grant to 'the German lad' as the cartoonists called him. Accordingly the Tories were able to take their revenge for the slights put upon them by refusing to vote more than £30,000. Another mortification for the Queen was that her uncles, the royal dukes, refused to concede precedence to her consort. There was trouble too because in her Declaration to Parliament to marry Melbourne had omitted to include any reference to the Prince's Protestantism and the Tories made capital out of this omission to suggest that it had been deliberately done to placate O'Connell. So Victoria found herself continually thwarted and Melbourne found himself powerless to help her.

But, though she raged at the insults offered to her 'beloved Albert', Victoria had no intention of allowing him to play any active part in the running of her country. Here she still relied on Melbourne; indeed in some ways the tie between them was never closer. She was in love with Albert and happy at the prospect of her marriage but Melbourne was the man at her side, her friend, her confidante, her counsellor and her second father. She was happy on Christmas Day because he took communion with her, being always a little uncertain as to how much importance he attached to religious observance. She still fussed over his health, recorded his jokes and amusing ways, wanted him near her. Rather touchingly, when she noticed that his writing-case was old and shabby she made him a present of a new one. On one occasion she told him that she was sure none of his friends were as fond of him as she was. Experienced in the ways of the world as he was he could not but know that with marriage this sweet intimacy must go, that though politically he would remain her closest adviser, she would no longer rely on his company in the long evenings at Windsor and the Palace; she would have a husband to ride out with her. Even fathers, however beloved, give place to husbands in happy marriages and his wish for her happiness was totally sincere. Meanwhile, like any father, he had a new and splendid dress coat made for the ceremony, sympathised with her last-minute nervous fears, telling her that they were only natural and that for a woman to marry was right, though he admitted that it did mean great changes and that, like everything else, it had its inconveniences. During the actual ceremony Lord Melbourne in his 'fine new dress coat' stood near her, bearing the Sword of State, as he had stood beside her at her coronation three years ago. In her journal that night she wrote how moved he was, and how later, when she went up to change into her going-away dress, Lord Melbourne came up to say goodbye and stayed with her half an hour. As any child and father might have done, the pair talked of how well everything had gone off. Then he kissed her hand, she in return pressed his and with a murmured 'God Bless you, Ma'am' and a last kind look he left her. A few minutes later she drove off with Albert 'Alone'. A new chapter was beginning for her; an old one ending for him.

Nevertheless for another year the Queen continued to depend on Melbourne. Much as she adored her 'beloved Albert' she never forgot that she was Queen. Indeed she returned to London after the shortest of honeymoons at Windsor on the grounds that she could not be long from the seat of power. Her attitude towards her husband rather resembled that of a lately married business tycoon who, exhausted by his responsibilites, looked to his partner for relaxation when the day was over. Not only did she refuse to discuss public affairs with her husband, she and Melbourne made quite sure that he remained within the Whig fold by insisting that they choose his Household for him and that George Anson, who until then had been Melbourne's own secretary, should now act in that capacity for the Prince. With her husband a prisoner of the Whigs there was little likelihood that while Melbourne remained Prime Minister his close relationship with the Queen would be seriously eroded. How long he could remain so was becoming increasingly problematical. The Cabinet was at sixes and sevens and Melbourne gave very little impression of caring about what policy was adopted as long as he could somehow keep his motley administration from falling apart. On 26 September Victoria, who was pregnant, wrote beseeching him to avoid a crisis, saying that any agitation at the moment might make her seriously ill. Unfortunately diplomatic crisis cannot always be accommodated even to royal pregnancies and by October Melbourne had to warn Victoria that the differences of opinion in the Cabinet between Palmerston and Lord John over the handling of Mehemet Ali were so great that he feared they might bring his administration down. This particular crisis was overcome but there were others. Palmerston was anxious to protect British interests in China; hostilities broke out; the navy went in, finally capturing Chusan. The unsettled state of Afghanistan, after the replacement of the ambitious Dost Mahomed by the more subservient Shah Sooja, continued to constitute a threat to peace in that part of the world, while at home the Cabinet was split over the question of Army discipline. No wonder that by January Melbourne, half thinking aloud (a somewhat disconcerting habit of his), told Lord Clarendon 'In all my experience, I never remember such a state of things; I never remember in the course of my political life, anything at all like it – it can't last – it's impossible this Government can go on.'

What eventually led to its collapse was not so much the dissensions within the Cabinet as the state of the national finances. The economy was depressed; unemployment was widespread; Chartist discontent was rumbling in the provinces; revenue was falling. Drastic new measures were needed to invigorate the economy and tap new sources of revenue but neither Melbourne nor his colleagues, in spite of a last minute change of the Chancellor of the Exchequer, when Baring the merchant banker replaced Spring Rice, were the men to produce them. Nevertheless something had to be done. The Government was not strong enough to re-introduce the unpopular income tax, Pitt's war time expedient that had been abandoned at the conclusion of peace, and the limits of indirect taxation had plainly been reached. Free-trade theories were in the air and it was decided to reduce the duties on both timber and sugar in the hope that the lower price would lead to a greater consumption and therefore in the long run more revenue. There was, however one serious obstacle to the adoption of such a solution. It involved a reduction in the price of slave-grown sugar and this brought the strong Abolitionist lobby out in opposition. Melbourne and his colleagues were well aware that their proposals were hazardous and that they might be rejected by the Commons and, looking ahead to that possibility, discussed seriously whether in that eventuality the Government should resign immediately or ask for a dissolution and appeal to the country. Melbourne was in favour of resigning on the grounds that the country was turning against the Whigs. Even the policy now advocated by Lord John, of substituting a fixed duty on corn imported into Britain in place of the existing sliding scale, Melbourne thought might lose them more votes in the country than gain for them in the manufacturing towns. The majority of his colleagues and indeed the Queen herself, once the battle had been joined, favoured a dissolution. With his customary loyalty to his friends Melbourne acquiesced, saying 'Of course I felt I must go on with them; and so we shall go on, bring in the old sugar duties, and then, if things are in a pretty good state, dissolve.' To Greville this decision wore a different look. In his eyes 'Melbourne's weak vacillating mind has been over-persuaded and he consents to do what he so hugely disapproves.' It was not the first time that his loyalty had overridden his judgement. When therefore, the Government, having refused to resign over the sugar duties, was defeated on a motion of no confidence moved by Sir Robert Peel on 5 June, Melbourne asked, against his better judgement, for a dissolution.

Between June and August, when the results of the election became known, the Queen demonstrated her confidence in her Prime Minister by paying a visit to Brocket where Melbourne entertained her and the Prince in style. The defeat of the Whigs at the polls made it clear that the country did not share her confidence. Instead the voters agreed with Peel's scathing question 'Can there be a more lamentable picture than that of a Chancellor of the Exchequer seated on an empty chest – by the side of a bottomless deficiency – fishing for a budget?' and returned the Tories with a majority of 78. It was the end of Melbourne's almost uninterrupted eleven years in office, first as Home Secretary and then as Prime Minister. From the beginning of the year he had realised that the end was very near and had been working steadily to make the break as easy as he could for the Queen, who on his resignation wrote to her Uncle Leopold that to lose him was the heaviest trial that she had ever had to endure. And, though she remained confident that 'God in His mercy will support and guide me through it all' , she added with an oblique note of reproach to the Almighty, that 'I feel that my constant headaches are caused by annoyance and vexation.' Nevertheless the semi-farce of the Bedchamber crisis was not to be repeated. For this both Melbourne and the Prince must take some credit. When Melbourne, as early as May, came to realise that even a dissolution would only postpone and not avoid his resignation he and the Prince, who was at last taking a more positive part in the background, with the help of George Anson, once his resented and now his valued private secretary, entered into a secret negotiation with Peel to sort out the vexed question of the Queen's 'Ladies' in advance. Even more fundamental was Melbourne's insistence to the Queen that in her own husband she had a wise counsellor with whom she could discuss her political questions. In the intervening months since her marriage, partly because of her early pregnancy and partly through the efforts of Anson and Melbourne, the Prince had been eased into a position of less political impotence and his coonsequence had been further enhanced by his having been designated as prospective Regent should Victoria die before their daughter, the Princess Royal, reached her majority.

Deeply, therefore, though Victoria grieved at the loss of her old friend she was no longer inconsolable, and was able, with the help of Melbourne's loving tact and the support of her husband to accept with resignation, and even composure, Sir Robert Peel and his Tory hordes. Melbourne too, at least outwardly, appeared resigned. When he told the Queen how deeply he felt the pain of no longer being able to continue in her service 'which had been no less his pleasure than his pride' he spoke with deep sincerity yet, like many men whose loss is known but has not yet been experienced, once the painful adieu had been made his spirits rallied. Emily described how he had then gone on to a cheerful dinner party at Carlton House where he and his close associates had all been 'very merry' as they talked over the latest events and criticised the new appointments. At least temporarily he must have felt the reaction of relief that the strain was over, the issue decided and that at last he could relax and enjoy the spring at Brocket free from official cares. It was only later that the full realisation of the emptiness of the future dawned.

To some extent even this was postponed by Victoria's determination not to allow politics to deprive her of either his company or his advice, though this determination was to place him in a difficult and ambiguous situation. The Queen had made it quite clear to Peel that she intended to continue to see Melbourne as an old friend, to which he had assented, and she interpreted this relationship very widely, so that it entailed much interchange of letters and much asking of advice on questions on which it was of doubtful propriety to consult a man who was now leader of the Opposition. Her other old friend and adviser, Baron Stockmar, was most alarmed lest this correspondence should become known to Peel, and both through Anson and in person he remonstrated with Melbourne. It is possible that Greville was displaying a sounder instinct when he wrote 'The best thing she (the Queen) can possibly do is to continue in her confidential habits with him as far as possible, for I am persuaded he will give her sound and honest advice; he will mitigate instead of exasperate her angry feelings, and instruct her in the duties and obligations of her position . . . and it is my firm conviction that he will labour to inspire her with just notions and sound principles and as far as within him lies will smooth difficulties which would be apt to clog her intercourse with his successor.' It was a fair assessment. In everything Melbourne wrote or did his only object was to make the change as easy for the Queen as possible and Peel can be considered lucky to have an opponent who was as anxious as himself that the Queen's Government should meet with no unnecessary obstacles. In any case so long as the Queen needed him he was hers to command and in the early days of September few went by without the interchange of letters. As leader of the Opposition her ex-Prime Minister was pleased by this reliance on him in an equivocal position, though he tried to shut his eyes to it, exploding with damns and expletives when it was suggested to him that it was undesirable that he should accept any invitation to visit Windsor, which by October Victoria was anxious to send to him, at a time when he was speaking against her official Government in the Lords. Undoubtedly at first she missed his daily presence and was eager to see him again. When writing to her Uncle Leopold on 8 September she commented sadly that the last eleven days was the longest time she had ever passed without seeing him. To Melbourne, bereft at once of her society and the occupation of office, adjusting to a new way of life must have been difficult, and the fact that Victoria at once needed and missed him was a great source of comfort to him. Apparently Melbourne paid no heed to Stockmar's horrified remonstrances; however but by the end of December Anson noticed that the interchange of letters was becoming less frequent and less concerned with politics. Victoria, immersed in her duties and her family, and relying more and more on Albert, was learning to share her husband's appreciation of Peel and to live without Lord Melbourne.

In any case his political life was almost over. Never a committed party man, during his early months in opposition he had tried to moderate Whig attacks on the Tories in order to make the transition as painless and problem-free for the Queen as possible, but how long he could have continued to influence such forceful colleagues as Palmerston and Lord John Russell must have been doubtful even if Nature had not intervened. Late in 1842 he had a slight stroke, and though he made a nominal recovery – indeed he supposed his disabilities to be due to a severe attack of lumbago – henceforth he was an old man. Victoria was much distressed. When after his recovery the Normanbys, who had been spending a few days at Windsor, went down to visit him at Brocket she asked them to give her a full account of his state of health, while later she sent Anson down to make a personal report. Gradually he recovered and by February 1843, to the dismay of his family who knew he was in no state to undertake such exertion, he wanted to return to his place in the Lords. Nevertheless he persisted in going up to London, only once there to realise his own inability to stand the strain of a parliamentary session. By the end of the year he was making a gallant effort to pick up the threads of his old life. Greville, who saw him in early December 1843 at Holland House, thought 'He looked tolerably well in the face but was feeble and out of spirits. He had been in the Queen's party at Chatsworth, which excited him and was bad for him. At first he made an effort to talk in his old strain; but it evidently was an effort, he soon relapsed into silence and was in a hurry to get away the moment dinner was over.' At times he could still exercise his old charm when dining with old friends or entertaining them at Brocket, but his old bouts of exuberant talkativeness, when he had held a table in thrall, were more and more infrequent. Gone were the days when, dining at Holland House, 'his laugh was frequent and the most joyous possible and voice so deep and musical that to hear him say the most ordinary things was a pleasure; but his frankness, his freedom from affectation and his peculiar humour, rendered almost everything he said, though it seemed perfectly natural, yet quite original.'

It was difficult to fight back. In February 1843 he complained to Victoria of sleeplessness, loss of appetite and wrote that the left side of his body was very much affected, yet he found it difficult to accept the fact that he was no longer either at the centre of power nor the centre of her attention. Her letters when they came were his greatest pleasure, reminding him as they did of the days when he had the honour and pleasure of serving her. But they came less and less frequently so that on one occasion he even permitted himself to confess to annoyance at her long silence. He still could not bring himself to accept the fact that he would never again play a major role in politics. When he wrote to her in the April of 1844 he admitted that he knew it was wrong to be impatient and to repine but that to accept the change from strength to weakness was hard and disagreeable. Sometimes he would lie awake wondering what advice he would give her if the Government fell and the Queen sent for him. It was a dream world that helped to blunt the edges of reality and which impelled him to 'assume an air and language as if he were the same man, and was ready to to act his old part on any stage and at any time'. But if he would not permit himself to realise the illusive nature of such dreams both the Queen and his ex-colleagues were very conscious of his failing powers. When Peel resigned, after his first attempt to carry the repeal of the Corn Laws in 1845 she was forced, very gently, to disillusion him. Her first impulse, she wrote, had been to invite him to come to Cowes, where she then was, so that she could have the benefit of his advice and assistance and, she went on, it was only the fear that his health would not be able to sustain the burden of office that had made her hesitate to ask him to resume his old one. This she assured him was her sole reason for sending for Lord John Russell when her confidence was still unabated in Lord Melbourne. To such a letter there was only one possible reply; with composed acceptance Melbourne thanked the Queen for her kindness and consideration while explaining with dignity that in view of his known opposition to a repeal of the Corn Laws it would have been difficult for him to head an administration pledged to repeal them. As Lord John failed to form a government Peel resumed office, carried the controversial repeal legislation and was defeated the same night by his furious colleagues who combined with his opponents against a government-sponsored Irish bill. When Peel resigned in the June of 1846 once again Melbourne dreamt of a return to office and when it was clear that no such offer would be made he wrote to Anson expressing his disappointment at having been passed over. Once again his old colleagues did their best to soften the blow and he was assured that Lord John would have liked to offer him the Privy Seal had it not been for concern over his health. Once again Melbourne stifled his hopes with dignity, writing on the 21st to the Queen in such a way as to imply that the lack of an invitation had been in response to his having made it clear, once he had seen that the fall of Peel's administration was imminent, that his health would not have been sufficiently good for him to have accepted even subordinate office. It was the end of his last hope of returning to Westiminster and once again enjoying his old relationship with the Queen.

Only two more years of life, which lassitude and boredom made seem very long, remained to him. Most of his time was spent at Brocket but now that he could no longer ride and shoot he found little to amuse him. Most of his life had been spent in London, with Brocket no more than a pleasant interlude where he could relax, but he was never a countryman at heart; though unlike Victoria, he liked the cawing of the rooks, he once told her that even the flowers bloomed better in London. Emily had always feared boredom for him, describing him as being unamusable, and dreading, even before it happened, the ennui and apathy that she knew must descend on him once his life had lost its purpose and drive. Since 1837 Victoria had been the main spring of his activities and his thoughts. In spite of his casual, detached manner his affections were deep and concentrated: his mother, Caroline, for a time Lady Brandon possibly, Mrs Norton and the young Queen, each in turn had held the centre of his stage. Now the stage seemed empty once the heroine was no longer there to fill it, though his friends and family did their best to entertain him. Emily came over frequently from Broadlands, his brother Frederick with his young Austrian wife spent long periods at Brocket. While he had still had reasonable health and could visit London the emptiness of his emotional stage was less apparent. Though Lord Holland had died in 1840 the indefatigable Lady Holland still gave her old dinner parties at which he was a welcome guest. He began to see Mrs Norton again, though with her grievances and sorrows she was a poor substitute for Victoria. Even when his health restricted him to Brocket old friends came down on short visits when for brief intervals his old animation seemed to come back, though Lady Holland's appearances were a mixed blessing as she, in her masterful way, was apt to turn the house upside down. Occasionally too there was a treasured letter from Victoria. Nevertheless the days dragged and the intrusions of the outside world seemed perhaps less frequent to the bored old man than in fact they were. Brooding and with too much time to think he worried about his finances. He had never been a very good manager; South Street had been expensive to rent and extravagant to run. Since his retirement he had been selling off some of the farms on his estates; as his health deteriorated his brother, trying to sort out the tangle of his finances, discovered that he spent as much as £700 a year on his doctors; he still made an allowance to Lady Brandon. By the end of December 1847 he confided to the Queen his worry that he would go bankrupt, telling her that it was his poor financial position that had forced him to decline the offer of the Garter when it had been made to him first by William IV and then by Victoria herself, though pride in serving without reward had in fact helped in that decision. Here at least was something concrete which the Queen felt she could do for her old friend, and through the ever useful Anson she placed a considerable sum at his disposal. That Melbourne had worried himself to a large extent unnecessarily, and that his affairs were by no means as desperate as he thought, does not detract from Victoria's generous wish to come to the assistance of the man who had once been of such assistance to her, though comparing her happiness then with that she now enjoyed with Albert it seemed a very inferior thing. But for Melbourne until the end of his life his memories were his constant companions and at the mere mention of her name his eyes would fill with tears. Then in the dark November days of 1848 he was taken dangerously ill with what were described as convulsive fits which for two days racked him. About six o'clock on the afternoon of the 25th, quite peacefully, he died. Both Emily and her husband Lord Palmerston were there until the end and it was he who wrote to tell the Queen on the 26th.

The Queen was saddened by the news, which came like an echo of the past from which the glamour had long departed. In writing to Leopold to give him the news she referred to the man who had given her so much devotion, and on whose affection and care she had once so completely relied, as 'our poor old friend' and her judgement looking back was that 'he was truly attached to me, and though not a firm Minister, he was a noble, kind hearted and generous being'.

However just her tribute to his personal qualities her assessment of him as a Minister, used as she was since his resignation to the more positive qualities of Peel and Lord John Russell, was something less than fair to his achievements as a politician. It is true that he never believed that society could be improved by legislation, however well intentioned; that he accepted the status quo, with all its inequalities and hardships, with equanimity; that he had no conception of what today is described as 'social justice'. But in the eighteen thirties, when reformers and die-hards were locked in bitter conflict, there were advantages in having a minister who was never partisan, a man who with courtesy and good temper could hold the ring. Change he found uncongenial but he realised that sometimes it had become politically unavoidable and when he yielded to the mounting pressure of public opinion he did so generously and honestly. He fought for the Reform Bill in the Lords with all the persuasive, reasonable arguments he could put forward. In the same way he gave full support to the Municipal Corporations Act of 1835, telling the Lords that 'with respect to the corporations it has always been my own strong and sincere opinion that a thorough reform of them was required'. Moreover it can be argued that by 1834 Britain had already been given such a rich diet of reforms that the country needed time to digest the new and important legislation that had already been passed, without adding to the list. Again Melbourne has been frequently arraigned for his blindness to social problems but it is far from clear whether any government at that time had either the experience or the machinery to carry out changes that would have materially improved the condition of the mass of the people. In any case the first effective Factory Act, that of 1833, and the controversial Poor Law Amendment Act of 1834 were passed while he was Home Secretary, though in neither case did the initiative come from him. Sceptical as he was of the benefits to be derived from governmental action he had very little sympathy with 'do-gooders' like Lord Ashley. Judging by the few members who by speaking or lobbying supported this type of legislation, Melbourne in his indifference was representative of the majority in their desire to leave well alone what to them was hallowed by custom.

Nor should the constitutional importance of his premiership be disregarded. During his life the balance of power was slowly shifting from the Crown in favour of Parliament and parties were beginning to take their more modern form. They were better organised, both in Parliament and in the constituencies, and they gave more regular support to recognised party leaders. It was to the changing position of the Crown rather than to party that Melbourne made his most useful contribution. It was his role, by tact and courtly deference, to ease these years of transition first for William IV and then for Victoria. Head-on clashes had to be prevented, difficult situations avoided, distasteful policies made to seem acceptable. For this task Melbourne was supremely fitted. Victoria's backward-looking judgement was that he lacked firmness and to some extent this was true. Betrayed partly by weariness and partly by affection, on critical occasions he could never be firm with her. She dominated the Bedchamber crisis, by her own resentment caused the Lady Flora scandal, and dictated their continued correspondence after his resignation; and where she led he followed. But with William IV he could be firm. According to Hobhouse Melbourne 'knew how to deal with his Master as well as with his colleagues, and never that I saw made a mistake in regard to either. I must add, that when a stand was to be made on any thing considered to be a vital principle of his government he was as firm as a rock', a quality that he also showed in his determined exclusion of Brougham from office.

Melbourne was on occasion baffled, and, seeing both sides of a problem, did nothing, but his vacillation did not spring from weakness. Moreover it can be argued that a less conciliatory premier would never have held so miscellaneous a team together while Victoria was learning the craft of kingship and until the country was ready for the positive leadership of Sir Robert Peel. In Church matters too he played a moderating part at a time when the church was under attack from the Evangelicals, from the Dissenters and from the Radicals. It was during his premiership that the Church of England was given the machinery by which it could put its own house in order and by his choice of good middle-of-the-road bishops he saved it from being torn by the dissensions of extremists. When Melbourne lay dying Lord Palmerston in his letter to the Queen told her that he was engaged in the melancholy occupation of watching 'the gradual extinction of the lamp of life of one who was not more distinguished by his brilliant talents, his warm affections and his first-rate understanding, than by those sentiments of attachment to your Majesty which rendered him the most devoted servant who ever had the honour to serve a Sovereign'. It is a fitting epitaph for a man who, whatever his faults, was supremely loyal to his family, his wife, his friends and his Queen.

SELECT BIBLIOGRAPHY

Byron, Lord *Correspondence chiefly with Lady Melbourne* (edited by J. Murray) 1822

Cecil, Lord David *The Young Melbourne* 1934
Lord M. 1954

Cooper, L. *Radical Jack* 1959

Greville C. *Memoirs* (edited by H. Reeves) 1874-80
Selection from the *Diaries* edited by P.W. Wilson in 2 vols. 1927
Memoirs edited in 8 vols by L. Strachey & R. Fulford. 1938

Guedella, P. *The Duke* 1931

Hobsbawn, J. & Rude, G. *Captain Swing* 1969

Jenkins, E. *Lady Caroline Lamb* 1932

Leverson Gower, *Private Correspondence 1781-1821* (edited by Castalia, Countess Glanville) 1916

Longford, Elizabeth *Wellington: Pillar of State* (1972)

Macintyre, A. *The Liberator* 1965. (A life of Daniel O'Connell.)

Marshall, D. *Industrial England 1776-1850.*

Morgan, Lady *Autobiography* (edited by W.H. Dixon) 1862

Newman, B. *Lord Melbourne* 1930

Ogilivy, M.F.E., Countess Arlie *In Whig Society* 1921
Lady Palmerston and her Times 1922

Perkins, J.G. *Life of Mrs Norton* 1909

Prest, J. *Lord John Russell* 1972

Quennell, P. *Byron: the Years of Fame* 1935

164

Ramsey, A.A.W. *Sir Robert Peel* 1928
Ridley, J. *Palmerston* 1970
Saunders, L.C. *The Melbourne Papers* 1889
 The Holland House Circle 1808
Torrens, W.M. *Memoirs of William Lamb, 2nd Viscount Melbourne* 1890
Queen Victoria *The Girlhood of Queen Victoria* 1912
 Letters, 1st series 1837-61 (edited by A.C. Benson & G.E. Buckle) 1907

BIBLIOGRAPHICAL NOTE

Much material concerning Lord Melbourne is contained in L.C. Saunders' *The Melbourne Papers* and in W.M. Torrens' *Memoirs of William Lamb, 2nd Viscount Melbourne* but these, published in 1889 and 1890 respectively, are no longer easily available and are, in any case, of a somewhat formal and semi-official character. The best and most sympathetic study of Lord Melbourne is to be found in Lord David Cecil's delightful two volumes, *The Young Melbourne* and *Lord M*. Rather more conventionally political in its treatment is B. Newman's *Lord Melbourne*. Much scattered information about Melbourne and his friends is contained in collections of contemporary letters, many of which have been edited and are available at least in libraries. Important among these are Leverson Gower, *Private Correspondence 1781-1821*, edited by Castalia, Countess Glanville, and *In Whig Society* and *Lady Palmerston and her Times*, both edited by M.F.E. Ogilivy, Countess Arlie. Lord Byron's *Correspondence chiefly with Lady Melbourne* edited by John Murray does much to illuminate their respective attitudes towards Lady Caroline Lamb, while her own point of view is contained in her letters to Lady Morgan which are to be found in the latter's *Autobiography* edited by W.H. Dixon, which however is not easily available as it was published in 1862. The Memoirs of Charles Greville are a valuable source of both fact and political gossip. Originally edited by Henry Reeves between 1874-80 these have been re-edited in eight volumes by L. Strachey and R. Fulford, but a shorter version of the *Diaries* edited by P.W. Wilson is also available for modern readers. Invaluable because of their personal angle are Queen Victoria's own journals and letters contained in *The Girlhood of Queen Victoria* and in the first series of her *Letters* covering the period 1837-69, edited by A.C. Benson and G.E. Buckle.

Biographies of people who played an important part in Melbourne's life include a sympathetic study by Elizabeth Jenkins of *Lady Caroline Lamb,* Jane G. Perkins' *Life of Mrs Norton,* and *Byron: the Years of Fame* by P. Quennell. For his political associates, John Prest in *Lord John Russell* gives an understanding picture of Lord John and is particularly useful filling in the political background of the period. Jasper Ridley concentrates on foreign policy in his study of Palmerston. Lady Longford has published two volumes on Wellington and P. Guedella's *The Duke* is lively and readable. N. Gash has only dealt with Sir Robert Peel's career up to 1830 in *Mr Secretary Peel* but for the later period A.A.W. Ramsey's *Sir Robert Peel* provides a useful account of that statesman's political life. The most modern biography of Lord Durham is Leonard Cooper's *Radical Jack* while Angus Macintyre provides a good up-to-date life of Daniel O'Connell under the title of *The Liberator.* Useful books dealing with the background of the period rather than with particular persons are L.C. Saunders, *The Holland House Circle,* of which Melbourne was a prominent member, *Captain Swing* by J. Hobsbawn and G. Rude which provides a detailed and sympathetic picture of the agrarian troubles with which Melbourne had to deal when Home Secretary, and my *Industrial England 1776-1850,* which aims at giving a non-specialist account of the general social and economic developments during the period covered by Lord Melbourne's life.

INDEX

169